In a Cheesemaker's Kitchen

This book is dedicated
to Sandy Reese and
Don Hooper, who have
cheered for us, pushed
us, scolded us, and
believed in us.

LIBRARY OF CONGRESS CATALOGING-IN-PUBLICATION DATA

ISBN 978-0-615-26205-5

Copyright © 2009 by Allison Hooper
and Vermont Butter & Cheese Company

All Photographs by Becky Luigart-Stayner, Sunny House Studio,
unless otherwise noted

Book design and composition by Steve Wetherby
and Tina Christensen, Scuola Group

Distributed to the trade by The Countryman Press, P.O. Box 748,
Woodstock, VT 05091, a division of W. W. Norton & Company, Inc.,
500 Fifth Avenue, New York, NY 10110

Mixed Sources
Product group from well-managed
forests, controlled sources and
recycled wood or fiber
www.fsc.org Cert no. SW-COC-001558
© 1996 Forest Stewardship Council
FSC

Printed in the USA
by Villanti & Sons, Printers, Inc.

10 9 8 7 6 5 4 3 2

A heartfelt thank you to all who have participated
in making this dream book a reality:

Photographer and owner Becky Luigart-Stayner of Sunny
House Studio for her splendid light and exquisite eye.

Steve Wetherby and Tina Christensen of Scuola Group for
their clean, attractive, imaginative design.

Writer Rebecca Davison for her inspired interviews with chefs.

Chefs Extraordinaire: Eric, Michel, Alison, Andrew, Raymond,
Mireille, Molly, and Dan for their generosity and confidence
in our life's work.

Food Eminence Steve Jenkins for his humor and candor.

Karen Daseke Peterman for recipe writing and testing;
Fonda Shaia, prop stylist, Jan Moon, food stylist; Bob Eddy
and Tim Calabro of First Light Studios for photos of farmers
and animals; Bastien Juif and Jon Hrichak for photos
of cheesemaking.

The farmers who nurture their animals every day of the year
and whose commitment doesn't allow too far an escape
between milkings. Thanks also to Keith Sprague, Marcel
Booth and bulk truck drivers Butch Lamberti and Ray Pouliot.

Don Larose, Kim Danforth, and our dedicated employees,
whose allegiance to making the best award-winning cheese
keeps our customers eager for more.

Our community of angels, bankers, Carl Thomas, Vermont
Agency of Agriculture, fellow food artisans, Vermont Cheese
Council, Vermont Fresh Network, American Cheese Society

Loyal food mavens: distributors, retailers, chefs, writers,
cheesemongers, and home cooks who took a chance.

Monumental tribute is due Adeline Druart, who
brought life to this book. Her exuberance and
perfectionism is evident on almost every page.
Without her big vision, steadfast management,
and inestimable *quelque chose,* this silver anniversary
gift to ourselves might have languished in the
ripening room for another decade.

In a Cheesemaker's Kitchen

ALLISON HOOPER

CELEBRATING 25 YEARS OF ARTISANAL CHEESEMAKING & COOKING
FROM VERMONT BUTTER & CHEESE COMPANY

Contents

Bob Eddy

Foreword

I was just asked by a journalist for a major magazine to name the cheese I most crave, but that I can't import for legal reasons. My immediate reaction was to tell her that there just aren't any foreign cheeses I long for anymore because superb American artisanal cheesemakers make all of them; and in most cases, each of these American cheeses is just as good or better than the cheese being emulated. So the journalist says, well, if that's the case, if that's really how you feel, then you and your Fairway Markets are just not going to appear in this article that will be read by x millions of people. So I rear back and move the telephone mouthpiece a few inches farther from my big mouth and go on to postulate that journalists such as yourself should think about supporting the home team here, and stop already with the Euro-worship, because those days are over, gone, and tiresome anyway. And that if she would simply place a Vermont Butter & Cheese Crottin beside one of Pascal Jacquin's AOC (*Appellation d'Origine Contrôlée*) Crottins de Chavignol from just outside Sancerre in the lovely Loir et Cher region of France called Berry, and if she would also have a tranche of crusty bread and a glass of a Sancerre rosé close to them, and if she would then cut both crottins with a handsome and rustic knife, slather them aboard the bread, and then take a sniff of both of these fromages de chèvre, taste both in turn, and follow them up with a slug of the wine, perhaps she would agree with me.

In fact, having performed just this exact procedure recently, I would have, should have, told this writer, "Hey! And guess what? I solidly prefer the VBC Crottin over the Jacquin one because the VBC goat cheese tastes more vivid, more primitive, rounder, deeper, nuttier, and spicier, with more toothsomeness, less gumminess, and a much more compelling, lingering finish than the French original, and I ought to know because I was the one who first brought AOC Crottins de Chavignol to the United States (New York City) for my cheese counters, back in, oh, 1980 or so.

Vermont Butter & Cheese has been around now so long that it does Allison and Bob a disservice to think of their dairy products as Frenchified or as European derivatives. So be it resolved by me that their butter, with or without sea salt, is so good as to provoke swoons, and that said butter blows away its competition, national and international, at every prestigious event at which they vie, and that it is made, like the masterly crottin, in a decidedly French style, using decidedly French techniques and tools, Vermont Butter & Cheese rules.

And I ought to know. I've been with them since the very beginning, and I have the magazine articles to prove it.

—**STEVE JENKINS**
Master Cheesemonger, Fairway Market

Opposite: Martha Rockwell herding her goats at Long Field Farm, Cabot, Vermont.

Preface   Mom and Beyond

Tim Calabro

In a Cheesemaker's Kitchen is a book about twenty-five years of surviving and thriving in a business doing what we love to do: make cheese for people who love food and love to cook. We have worked hard, and we have celebrated our work every day by cooking with our cheeses for our families who all have grown up in a generation that increasingly appreciates good food.

This book is not just about the food. It is also an opportunity to acknowledge a business partnership that has endured tough times and flourished into a great lifelong friendship. The words in this story are in my voice, but the partnership is implicit throughout. I may have had the good fortune to travel to France, experience the food, and even make some cheese, but without Bob Reese, this business would never have launched, much less succeeded. With his good humor, eagerness to please, and business smarts, we have built a career and livelihood from making cheese. He has taught me that good business is about balancing priorities and taking care of the many moving parts from farmers to customers, always challenging ourselves. For twenty-five years we have trusted the other's intuition for our distinct areas of interest and expertise — always questioning, never deserting, always loyal. The lives of our spouses and the six male offspring between us are inexorably tied to the synergies and differences, the yin and yang that is Vermont Butter & Cheese. I thank Bob for entrusting me to chronicle our adventure.

Mercifully, my mother was a wonderful cook. Every night when I was growing up, we ate supper as a family of five around a modest, traditional family dining table. The fare was simple and unpretentious, but delicious. Today, like a lot of nostalgic offspring, I follow my parents' wholesome, unspoken recipe for togetherness and respite from the swirl. My own family of five sits down over supper every night that we can. We celebrate our good luck and good health over simple good food that I fish from the fridge — nothing too fancy, but oh so tasty and satisfying. As you can imagine, goodies from Vermont Butter & Cheese Company figure prominently in my family's daily diet.

I look forward to my time in the kitchen each night, getting lost for just the thirty meditative minutes it takes to peruse the larder and inventory what's ripe in the summer garden. Then, hugging a colander of beet greens, an acorn squash, a clutch of parsley, some basil, perhaps a jalapeño pepper, a handful of green beans, some cherry tomatoes, or a spadeful of new potatoes, I color outside the lines. Whatever the homespun creation turns out to be, I always add my not-so-secret, never-fail cheese enhancements. It takes no more

Allison Hooper carresses a doe at Paula and Marcel Masse's farm in Craftsbury, Vermont.

than a crumbled chèvre log, a double dollop of crème fraîche, or a generous spoonful of sea salt butter to make some self-effacing pasta concoction sing and dance.

We're now in our twenty-fifth year of making delectable European-style specialty cheeses and butters in the bucolic hills known as Vermont's Green Mountains. Therefore, what better time than now, as an anniversary present to ourselves, to share our passion and some family secrets with devotees.

Over our quarter century, through a whole lot of fun experimentation, we've discovered some of the secrets of why our gastronomic memories of French cuisine are so robust and romantic and crave to be refreshed. Many of our products attempt to replicate the dairy staples available on French farms and in European markets that make everyday eating some sort of magic.

What a break for us that some of our most ardent, enthusiastic customers moonlight as the best chefs in the United States. What a compliment it is that this distinguished delegation of culinary pros volunteered eagerly to help us illustrate how best to enjoy our flavorful, down-to-earth, increasingly available products.

Some of our cheeses are new to American palates and want interpretation. When we started, there was hardly any fresh goat cheese or even crème fraîche on the menu in the United States. Today they're standard fare, boasting a burgeoning fan club. Not so, yet, for mascarpone, quark, and fromage blanc — to say nothing of our newest: slightly aged goat milk delicacies, Bijou, Coupole, and Bonne Bouche.

This was a book just itching to be written, languishing on our personal and professional wish list for way too long. We hope we've achieved our goal of introducing you to a few of our favorite ways to jazz up your food repertoire with cheeses that are celebratory, healthy, and easy to prepare. So raise a glass to help us celebrate our incredible first-quarter century. Please help us to toast our self-indulgent passion for transforming beautiful, wholesome fresh milk into some of the most delectable, sustainably produced cheeses in the world. Bon appétit!

—ALLISON HOOPER
April 2009

Opposite: Allison clutches the "house starter culture" in the first milk house creamery for a poster that hung at Bread & Circus, now Whole Foods Market, in Cambridge, Massachusetts, in 1986.

When I reflect, I marvel at the naive nerve Bob Reese and I had in 1984. Research would have told us there was no market for goat cheese in the United States, to say nothing of esoteric cultured products like quark, crème fraîche, and mascarpone. The cow farmers in my White River Valley of Vermont thought we were nuts, going hippie, tilting at windmills. Twenty-five years later, what began as a quaint creamery on a hill farm in Brookfield, Vermont, is today a national leader on the thriving artisanal cheese scene. In 2008, at the Fancy Food Show in New York City, Vermont Butter & Cheese Company (VBC) captured the coveted SOFI (Specialty Outstanding Food Innovation) Award for "Outstanding Product Line" — picked from among the five thousand chocolatiers and importers of foie gras and olive oils. This was a thrilling moment for us. This was a recognition we never dreamed we would achieve. "Who would have believed it?" Bob concedes, when he and I muse on our recipe for our improbable success—a pail of passion for cheesemaking, a pinch of instinct, a dash of heart, a snippet of vision, and a whole bunch of very good luck.

The SOFI is the "Oscar" of the food world.
National Association for the Specialty Food Trade

A SERENDIPITOUS BEGINNING

We found ourselves in the business of making cheese accidentally. The stars, however, ultimately aligned as we each brought complementary skills and a mutual passion for sustainable down-home agriculture. I brought a dream and the experience to make cheese, while Bob brought financial discipline, a fascination with agricultural sustainability, and the knowledge of how to sell good, wholesome food.

As a Connecticut College student studying in France, with no money to travel on my summer break, I worked on Jean and Lelia Lebras' hardscrabble farm in Brittany in exchange for room and board. From the Lebras, I learned to make an array of fresh and aged cow and goat milk cheeses, which they sold at farmers' markets on the coast and in Paris. What impressed me most was the way the French connect to their working rural landscape. I learned the intrinsic value of *terroir*, the harmony among place, culture, and food.

From his earliest memories, Bob thought he would one day take over his grandparents' dairy farm in the state of Washington. Unfortunately, before Bob finished high school in Vermont, they'd sold the far-away farm. But he just couldn't get the farm out of his blood. He earned an agribusiness degree at the University of Vermont and started his career marketing farm products for the Vermont Department of Agriculture.

Allison works a *ventilateur du grain* on the farm in France, a contraption that collects the seeds from the harvest to be planted for the next season, 1982.
VBC

Opposite: Framing Barbara Carter's original company sign, Bob Reese and Allison Hooper grin over their 25-year improbable business partnership.

VBC

VBC

Top: Bob and Allison proudly display their cheese and crème fraîche.

Bottom: Bob Reese and son Brendan demo cheese at the Hanover Consumer Coop, New Hampshire, 1989.

Appropriately enough, our improbable run as long-term business partners began in 1984 during a dinner celebrating Vermont agricultural products. It had been Bob's great idea to hold an awards banquet honoring restaurants that used Vermont products. But in the planning, as Bob retells the story, "I got a sinking feeling when Anton Flory, the chef at the Top Notch Resort in Stowe, asked me to get him goat cheese for a signature lamb dish he was preparing for the event. Where in the heck was I going to find goat cheese made in Vermont?" Bob then learned that a woman who was working at the state dairy lab could make goat cheese. That was me! And, of course, I said, "Sure I'd be happy to make some cheese." So we were both pretty proud that night when the compliments flowed in to Chef Flory for his lamb and goat cheese entrée.

After dinner, a few chefs left their business cards with me and asked how they might buy some cheese. I thought I'd fall over. I turned to Bob and said, "Well, what do I do now?" Bob didn't have an answer, but his wife Sandy did: "Why don't you two go into business together?"

Sandy's impulsive idea clicked. I remember the elation of fantasizing that my dream of a cheese business suddenly jelled. Across the table, Bob was chomping at the bit for the opportunity to stretch his marketing skills and test the reality of a soil-based venture.

We were decidedly short on capital, but we had determination, enthusiasm, and good instincts. We each brought $1,000 to the enterprise, and our first "angel," as our supporters would come to be called, was the United Church of Christ, which gave us a $4,000 loan. The money went toward renovating the small milk house on the farm in Brookfield and buying rudimentary cheesemaking equipment. We invested what we could scrape up and kept the bigger vision for the long term.

Our first product was chèvre, a fresh, mild cheese that wouldn't overpower the straightforward American palate. We tried to sell the goat cheese directly to consumers at rural farmers' markets, but in the 1980s, even eat-healthy customers just weren't that adventuresome, and words like "localvore" weren't yet part of the American vernacular. We realized we needed to sell in metropolitan markets like New York and Boston and to chefs who knew cheese. To do that, we had to build credibility with chefs that our cheese was as good as what they were importing. When we finally connected with the high-end chefs, it made all the difference—Vermont Butter & Cheese was up, producing, and poised to deliver when Americans eventually discovered artisanal cheeses.

Making a consistent, tasty cheese that had more than a two-day shelf life was tricky. But actually getting the goat milk was way-trickier. Bob and I cajoled backyard hobbyists to get licensed so they could sell their goat milk to us. We desperately needed milk. Bob remembers spending a lot of time driving around Vermont picking up a can of milk here and a can there. It was a constant battle to supply the chèvre our new customers demanded. And there were embarrassing moments, such as the time a chef called to order cheese for the following week. Bob had to tell him our tiny inventory was "sold out." Then the chef said, "Well, then I'll take

some butter." Bob had to tell him, "Well, we don't have any butter either." The guy was totally confused. "So, let me get this straight," he said to Bob. "You're the Vermont *No Butter & No Cheese Company?*"

The chronic shortage of goat milk in the early days drove us to think about adding a cow milk product. We decided on crème fraîche, a thick, slightly tart, creamy product that is a staple of French cuisine. I ate crème fraîche daily on the farm in Brittany. For dessert, the fermented raw cream topped a bowl of tangy fromage blanc. It was perfect. The source of the milk we would use was Marcel Booth, a small-creamery owner in Barre, Vermont and one of our "angels," who allowed me to come down every morning and pick up cans of his high-quality, high-butterfat cream.

MAKING THE DREAM HAPPEN WHILE LIVING IN THE REAL WORLD

By 1986, we had outgrown the Brookfield milk house. It was time to leave the farm and take a leap of faith by investing in an off-the-farm plant that would allow expansion of the product line. Periodically over the next two years I had the feeling we were either on the brink of euphoric surprising success or flaming predictable disaster.

Scrimping and cobbling together intermediate technology and retrofitted discarded equipment in our "new" plant, it felt like we were breaking all kinds of new ground. This new step wasn't like making cheese on that little farm in France. The United States has strict

In the foreground is the Brookfield "Milk House," the original VBC "plant." In the background is the barn that housed goats.

Original 1984 label by Bill Harvey of Burlington, Vermont.

Jeff Clarke

On winning the Vermont Business Persons of the Year award in 1996, Bob and Allison present Governor Howard Dean with an Alpine Kid while U.S. Senator Patrick Leahy brightens at not being so feted.

Allison bears a cheese basket for a feature in the food section of *The Boston Globe,* 2001.

Caleb Kenna, © Copyright 2001. *The Boston Globe.* Republished with permission.

regulations discouraging the use of raw milk. We had to pasteurize everything and figure out how to use starter cultures, which we never used in France. Because there was pretty much no one else in the United States doing what we were trying to do, we progressed largely through trial and error, with the emphasis on error.

And then there were the skeptics. The engineers who installed the equipment in the new plant looked at me like I was crazy. They tried to tell me I wasn't making cheese correctly. (They only knew how to make a hard cheese like cheddar.) When they saw what I pulled out of the fermentation tanks, they were doubtful because it was soft, like yogurt. They were sure we weren't going to survive. Despite financial and construction hurdles, and the skepticism about my cheesemaking ability, Bob and I successfully opened the new creamery in Websterville, Vermont, in 1988.

We also began to scoop up opportunities to craft new products. Bob noticed, for example, that during the holiday season specialty importers ran out of mascarpone, a sweet and savory, very rich, creamy cow milk cheese. I decided to design my own mascarpone. I was heartened that I was on the right track when the product was singled out by the *New York Times* as the only new and noteworthy cheese at the 1990 Fancy Food Show in New York. Bob was also ecstatic when our mascarpone was almost instantly picked up by a couple of New York restaurants.

Creamy goat cheese is another story of where we were able to spot a need, then stretched to meet it. On a visit to Sutton Place Gourmet in Washington DC, Bob was talking with Chef Dan Lewis, who happened to mention that he blended chèvre with fresh cow milk ricotta to make it creamy and smooth for lasagna. I immediately piped up with a suggestion that VBC try making the chèvre creamy and smooth for him.

We did make the product — Dan loved it, as did other chefs. The fresh, creamy goat cheese retains the tangy, slightly salty taste qualities chefs like, plus it can be piped through a pastry bag, spread on canapés, and added as a finish for sauces.

Oddly enough, it took us almost a decade to make the flagship product that is in our company's name — butter! Bob and I stumbled by accident onto a way to get butter into production. On one of our trips around Vermont searching for goat milk, we spotted a creaky, obsolete butter churn on the Weybridge town green and got Monument Farms to sell it to us for $3,000. I remember the first time we used it, the sides of the churn shook so violently we thought it was going to self-destruct. Called by one food critic, "the new grand cru," VBC's European-styled cultured butter is made with rich cream and allowed to ferment, which builds in a rich, full flavor. Incidentally, we are still using the sixty-year-old secondhand churn.

AIMING FOR PERFECTION

In 1996, the U.S. Small Business Administration honored us with its prestigious Vermont Business Persons of the Year award. In addition to going to Washington to meet President Clinton, we were required to host a celebratory bash. We decided to pair all nineteen cheesemakers in the state with nineteen top-notch Vermont chefs. It was a full-blown festival at Shelburne Farms. More than five hundred people attended, most commenting that they had no idea there were so many fine cheesemakers in Vermont. Working with the Vermont Agency of Agriculture and a handful of cheesemakers, this event became the catalyst that created the Vermont Cheese Council, which would position Vermont as the "Napa Valley" of artisanal cheese.

In the back of my mind I had always kept a vision of developing the traditional, small, rinded goat cheeses that flourish in France. Initial market success attracted skilled French interns to VBC. Just as I had been smitten by French cheese twenty years earlier, Adeline Druart, a French graduate student, was smitten by the American entrepreneurial spirit. From the National Dairy School in France, armed with talent and creativity, Adeline joined our Websterville, Vermont team in 2005. She earned her master's degree by designing the state-of-the-art ripening facility that helped perfect VBC's three unique, aged goat cheeses.

Reminiscent of the small, delicately ripened Crottins de Chavignol found in French open-air markets, VBC's Bijou epitomizes what is special about goat milk cheese. As Bijou ages, the interior becomes soft and the flavor robust. Similarly, our Bonne Bouche — literally "good mouthful"— is a hand-ladled, ash-ripened cheese that won first place for aged goat cheese at the 2001 American Cheese Society competition in Louisville, Kentucky. Shaped like a snow-covered dome, Coupole, an American original, creates a distinctive contrast between the strong, ripened flavor of the rind and the delicate, fresh taste of the interior.

Vermont Butter & Cheese's award-winning product line epitomizes the vision Bob and I had of introducing really good European-style artisanal cheese to American cheeseboards. While we made mistakes on the way to the market, we tried never to sacrifice quality or stop believing in our dream. Twenty-five years ago, I remember not having a persuasive rebuttal for a New York distributor who admonished us, "For God's sake, don't tell anyone that you are making cheese on a farm!" Bob and I dismissed the rebuke and, out of a passion for cheesemaking and a love of the land, we mercifully are a part of a food movement that has changed the American cuisine. ✂

French cheesemaker Adeline Druart tests her *savoir-faire* at the Websterville creamery.

Vermont Butter & Cheese Company's aged goat cheeses.

Bob Eddy

Jean Claude Roberge and daughter Chantal have been providing milk to us since 2005.

O f all the compelling ideas and old-world concepts that Vermont Butter & Cheese Company literally has lifted lock, stock, and barrel from our French mentors and imported unapologetically to American tables, the most important is the notion of *terroir*. "The taste of a place," *goût du terroir*, attributes the alluring, unique taste of each fine artisanal cheese to both the milking animals and to the surroundings in which they live. Nature and nurture together conspire to produce the desirable taste and consistency of the cheeses we make.

In May, when our animals cavort for the first time in the new season on the back-forty where red clover, Vermont's state flower, grows abundantly, it is easy to discern the sweet clover taste in our fresh milk. So too, with *terroir*, but its blend of contributors is more subtle and complicated. Vermont's climate, soil, geology, and pasture quality, as well as the specific grasses eaten by the individual breeds of goats, cows, and sheep, and additionally the character of the water the animals drink all contribute to the taste of a particular cheese. Ultimately, it is the skill of the herdsman and the attentiveness, know-how, and even passion of the farmer that are defining to the quality of the cheeses we produce.

When we began making goat cheese in 1984, sustainable family-farm goat dairying in Vermont was virtually nonexistent. But we knew that to succeed in the cheese business, we'd have to replicate the thriving goat industry we saw in France. Vermont's prized but anachronistic tradition of bucolic hill farms producing delicious, fresh cow milk was under pressure to survive. Squeezed by low milk prices while feed and equipment costs soared, the sixty-cow family farm was being forced to get bigger or get out. In 1960, expensive, "modern" stainless-steel bulk tanks for the rapid cooling and holding of fresh milk were made mandatory on all Vermont farms, including even the most marginal. By the '70s, village feed stores and

© istockphoto.com/fhyvler

John Deere tractor dealers were giving way to Troy-Bilt distributors and garden-supply franchises. Farm-animal veterinarians got supplanted by pet vets.

Relentlessly, the ten thousand family hill farms that characterized Vermont's working rural landscape in the 1950s morphed inexorably into much larger, allegedly more efficient, valley-bottom farms that milked a hundred or more cows rather than the thirty, fifty, or sixty-five Bessies of days gone-by.

But the small-scale caring tradition, the love of the land, even fortunately the land itself, remained— somewhat overgrown, but mostly undeveloped, thirsting for revival. We wondered aloud why dairy goats couldn't browse at least some fading farmsteads back to viability. After all, our snowy winter landscape still melted into a moist spring and temperate summer that made lush hillside pasture. For more than a century, grazed first by sheep, then by cows, Vermonters earned their honest living from herds of ruminants. What more appropriate, practical, good use of Robert Frost's tough, tilted, but verdant Vermont topography than *terroir* agriculture?

Dairy goats are intelligent, gregarious, and gentle. A mature doe will often give birth to twins. She'll then milk ten months of the year and give an average of two to four quarts of milk per day for up to a decade. As ruminants, goats require forages in the form of hay or pasture in addition to grain. Goats are fastidious, desiring clean and palatable food. They enjoy browsing on brush and a full spectrum of pasture plants. They are never tethered and enjoy nestling with the herd on their bedding hay, loafing and basking as the brilliant southern sun of a January snowscape pours into the recreation area of an open barn. In July, they can be found taking refuge en masse under a fence-line of sugar maples.

Melvin Lawrence greets a newborn kid on his farm in Shaftsbury, Vermont.

Bob Eddy

Five breeds — handsome Toggenburgs, feisty Alpines, needy Nubians, ear-challenged La Manchas, and milk-white Saanens — produce precious, gorgeous, and healthy milk. Like human milk, goat milk fat globules are small and naturally homogenized. They are easily digested and are often recommended for infants as an alternative to cow milk. In the 1970s, almost the only goat milk to be found in Vermont was from small, often backyard herds supplying their families with a fresh milk alternative to infant formula. These, and some other families who made a hobby of breeding and showing goats, supplied the first milk to the creamery.

Those few pioneering goat dairies grew almost overnight into a fledgling industry of five. Initially, we drove a Toyota pickup clear around the state picking up milk in ten-gallon cans. When that truck was at capacity, the farmers themselves brought us their milk. And when their trucks were full, we hired a mini–bulk truck to stop at each farm to collect the milk, as we still do today.

Challenges of profitability and sustainability confront all family farmers. Goat farmers are no exception. The long-term viability of our community of family farmers required us to make an infusion of technical assistance to help farms survive and prosper. To flourish, our small, milk-dependent, burgeoning cheese business committed itself to helping our farmers grow and improve their incomes. We certainly didn't have all of the answers, but we held out an audacious vision of former cow farmers dotting a renewed landscape with goats. Not unlike our goal of making the best cheese, we believed that if we helped our farmers solve problems, their desire for excellence would be infectious. Today our full-time, circuit-riding "goat nanny" spends her days in weathered barns and high pastures assisting farmers with ruminant nutrition, smart breeding, and milk quality. She dishes out sticky buns, hot coffee, belly laughter, and tough love in a state where a book titled *Real Vermonters Don't Milk Goats* is a popular seller.

Today, the smallest of the twenty-five farms supplying the creamery milks forty goats, and the largest, six hundred. The average farm milks two hundred goats. Former cow barns with small bulk tanks and modest milking parlors have been easily adapted for goats. A well-run commercial goat farm requires superb management and expertise to be successful. We pay our farmers a premium price to produce the high-protein, hormone-free, excellent milk that is essential to year-round cheesemaking. Without their *terroir* and sustainability, we wouldn't have a chance at making terrific chèvre. ✀

Bob Eddy

Our cream comes from the farmers of the St. Albans Cooperative Creamery near the Canadian border. Thanks to Ben & Jerry's and Stonyfield Farm, which buy St. Albans Creamery milk, these farmers pledge to produce milk that is free of growth hormones. In the spirit of Vermonters taking care of their neighbors, this progressive co-op sells us the fresh, high-butterfat cream needed to make superb butter, crème fraîche, and mascarpone. They're the best.

VBC

The Artisan In a Cheesemaker's Studio

Is what we do art, craft, science experiment, or just plain magic? For over a quarter century, we've digested how-to tomes, endured advanced chemistry courses, dozed through soft-ripened seminars, interrogated dyspeptic mentors, passed oppressive exams, and discarded some awful cheese — all in our quest to "get it right." And, after steeping ourselves in organic science and imbibing all the crafty art of cheesemaking esoterica, what are our conclusions?

Making really delicious cheese is like leading a Dixieland jazz band. A lot of players can toot an up-tempo horn, but getting the whole combo to swing outlandishly is something else again.

We take nature's most basic grocery, pristine fresh milk — what mammals lavish on their vulnerable infant offspring — and, under controlled conditions, turn it into sumptuous cheese, delicious and enduring.

A good cheesemaker manages milk quality and composition. We put together what we think is just the right combination of bacterial cultures to transform the milk. To the extent we can, we control the pH of the curd, the amount of salt, the various temperatures during different stages of the processing, the ladling technique, draining duration, and every aspect of the environment of the aging facility.

Each new cheese we produce is the product of months, sometimes years, spent trying to get it "just right". With each batch, we dissect, analyze, and adjust the recipe or "technology" to improve and eventually "perfect" our cheese. The more we control the circumstances of the intersection between curd and culture — the science of cheesemaking — the more we can indulge our expressive impulses when we add our proprietary *quelque chose*. Like the jazz band leader, we sometimes subtly nudge, sometimes overtly shove, our flavors and textures to where they make the music we want.

Artisanal cheesemakers do not standardize their milk. Unlike industrialists, we don't separate the fat and skim only to reassemble them later in an attempt to assure eaters that our inputs are identical every day of the year.

The *terroir* of seasonal changes, such as adjustments in animal feed and outdoor temperature, affect the composition of the milk we use for cheese. As our milk and cream change their character moderately from spring to summer or fall to winter, we, too, adjust our recipes and formulas for making the cheeses. For example, our butter is bright yellow

VBC

John Hrichak

Top: Adeline preparing fresh milk for cheesemaking.

Bottom: Freshly ladled cheese curds draining in their forms.

and soft during the summer when the cows are eating grass high in carotene, producing milk that is high in unsaturated fats. Winter butter is firmer, less vibrant, because the cows are eating stored forage. In the spring, our goat cheeses taste floral and have a consistency that is lighter and fluffier. Winter cheese is made with high-butterfat milk, which endows it with a rigorous creamy texture and imparts a richer, nutty flavor.

Our experience over many seasons of trying to accommodate nature's nuances allows us cheesemakers to infuse some creativity into our recipes for making signature cheeses. The great Yankee catcher and master of circular reasoning, Yogi Berra, is credited with the syllogism, "You can observe a lot just by watching." Obvious and sensible as Yogi's axiom may seem, we make a fetish of our adherence to it. By sniffing, fondling, and scrutinizing, we get our best information on whether this will be a great batch of cheese or just a good batch. We use humble observation as both a first and a sixth sense while witnessing the maturation we are trying to stimulate. By examining the texture of the curd and the color and clarity of the whey, we know best when it is time to ladle. We know well, too, that the cheeses will drain efficiently and age at just the right speed if we are careful to ladle the curd rhythmically, uniformly, and without breaking it.

The creamy winter goat cheeses, high in butterfat, need additional warmth in the make-room and extra time in the drying room. Cheeses move from drying room to aging room by touch rather than by the clock. The aroma in the aging room is our best assurance of a rightly wrinkled skin of a rind. Significantly, our noses tip us off to just how good we can expect the interior of that Bijou or Coupole to be. We use temperature, humidity, and pH recorders assiduously, but we get our most important information from our eyes, hands, and noses.

Americans who have been to France and come home craving a reminder of their magical European experience love our cheeses. If we've done nothing more than indulge their fantasies with our Vermont *terroir*, our cheesemaking *savoir-faire*, and our appetite for excellence, then these first twenty-five years will have been a magnificent success. ✃

Allison flipping Bijou
in the aging room.

Cow Milk——**Making Crème Fraîche and Cultured Butter**

Making crème fraîche begins with high-fat cream. After pasteurization, the cream is "set" in a tank where selected starter cultures are added to the tempered cream. During the maturation process, the culture metabolizes the lactose (milk sugar) into lactic acid. This takes about one full day, resulting in a full, rich flavor and thick texture.

Some crème fraîche is sent to the barrel churn where it takes thirty minutes to churn into butter. The buttermilk is drained until we reach the targeted 86 percent butterfat. To enhance the culture flavor we lightly salt the butter and package it in a log shape.

Goat Milk—

Making Fresh and Aged Goat Cheese

1. Pasteurization: To ensure that the milk is free of any harmful bacteria, we heat our fresh milk to 163°F as required in the U.S. for any cheeses consumed fresh (under sixty days of aging). The milk is cooled to the optimum temperature at which the starter cultures will work efficiently.

2. Maturation/Coagulation: Cultures are added to metabolize the lactose in the milk into lactic acid. The twenty-four-hour process allows the lactic acid to coagulate the liquid milk into a solid curd. A few drops of nonbovine coagulant are added to help form the curd.

3. Curd Ladling/Draining: When the curd reaches the right pH, we ladle the soft curd into perforated forms or into cloth bags, allowing the liquid whey to drain from the cheese for twenty-four hours.

4. Shaping: Once the curd is drained to the correct moisture, the soft curd is shaped into logs of fresh chèvre, domes for Coupole, or buttons for Bijou. The ladled curd is removed from the forms, and a coating of ash and salt is added to make Bonne Bouche.

5. Drying: Bonne Bouche, Coupole, and Bijou cheeses go to a warm, ventilated drying room for one to three days. We turn them daily to ensure uniform drying of the surface of the cheese.

6. Aging: The three cheeses develop their unique character and flavor in the aging room, where it is quiet, cool, and humid. The sought-after geotricum rind requires precise control of the environment. Slow rind development will produce the desired final moisture and flavor of the cheese. After one week, the cheeses are packaged in a wooden crate and wrapped in perforated film to allow them to continue to ripen and breathe until they reach your table.

John Hrichak, VBC, Bastien Juif, Sky Chalmers

Glossary

Ash comes from the poplar tree. It is sprinkled on the surface of the cheese to neutralize the surface acidity and allow the yeast and mold to grow and create the rind.

Geotricum rind is a yeast that grows on the surface of the cheese. The rind has a unique wrinkled appearance typical of the goat cheeses from the Loire Valley in France. It is delicious to eat.

pH is the measurement of acidity in the milk or cheese. Chèvre is a lactic curd cheese that has a low pH, giving it a tangy flavor when fresh.

Cow Milk Butter and Cream

Cultured Butter

Following the traditional French method of using real cultured cream, we churn and work the crème fraîche until the butterfat reaches 86 percent. Spread on a slice of good bread, this butter is practically a meal in itself. What's more, it is a delight to cook with because it can be heated to high temperatures. So when you pan sear your pork chop, it will neither burn nor absorb too much butterfat. For pie crust, VBC butter gives the dough elasticity, making it easier to roll out smoothly, and the crust is light and flaky.

Crème Fraîche

A staple of French cuisine, crème fraîche is made from fresh pasteurized cream that is fermented to obtain a rich texture and nutty flavor. It can be used as an ingredient for sauces, pastry, custard, or as a topping on pie, fruits, and soups.

How presumptuous of us to include butter in our name without a churn! A decade into the business there was still "no butter" until Bob and I spotted an appropriately sized churn resting in the dooryard of Monument Farms Dairy in Weybridge, Vermont. We drove around the square just long enough to muster up the courage to let ourselves in and make an offer to buy the churn.

Cow Milk Cheese—Fresh

Fromage Blanc

An everyday work-a-day cheese in France, fromage blanc is sold with varying amounts of fat. Ours is made with skimmed cow milk. Thicker than yogurt, this fat-free fresh cheese is a great source of protein and calcium. It can be topped with honey and fruits for a snack. Enlivened with fresh herbs, fromage blanc makes a delicious dip.

Quark

This German-style fresh cheese, similar to old-fashioned cream cheese, is from whole cow milk that slowly coagulates overnight. We drain the fresh curd through cheese cloth and whip it before it's packaged and shipped. Its low butterfat content and smooth texture make it a great base for fluffy cheesecakes and mousse. Top with granola for breakfast or mix with anything from mashed potatoes to boysenberries, and it earns its keep with flair.

Mascarpone

Mascarpone is the magic ingredient in the Italian dessert called tiramisu. This cream is cooked at a high temperature until it is thick, smooth, and sweet. The higher the butterfat content, the better. If you love it light and fluffy, whip it a tad, sweeten, and serve with fresh berries, or poached pears. Or right out of the tub, swirl it into soups or fold it into risotto and polenta; or mix it with Parmesan cheese and fill raviolis or layer it in lasagna. Versatile? You bet.

Creamy Goat Cheese

Created for Chef Dan Lewis at Sutton Place Gourmet in Washington DC, this smooth, fresh goat milk cheese is similar to goat milk ricotta. After overnight coagulation, the fresh curd is drained in a cheese cloth for one day and then whipped. The smooth texture makes it perfect to deploy in sauces, pasta fillings, spreads, or simply as a dip.

Chèvre

Chèvre means "goat" in French and is now used in the United States to describe fresh goat milk cheese. Our flagship chèvre was VBC's first product in 1984. We drain the goat milk curd for two days in cheese cloth and then shape it into logs that are sold fresh. Our chèvre has three personas: straightforward, classic colonial white; rolled in herbes de Provence forest green; and zesty red and green peppercorn.

Feta

Greek feta is a brine-cured fresh cheese made from ewe and goat milk combined. VBC feta follows the traditional Greek recipe, except that it is made with 100 percent goat milk. To keep the fresh milk taste in the cheese, keep the brine low in salt. Feta transforms a mesclun mix salad and transports you to the agora for a supper with Socrates when used in a phyllo-based spinach pie.

Fresh Crottin

Fresh Crottin is a young goat cheese that benefits from a special yeast and mold added to the milk to enhance the flavors. The cheese is fresh with a great citrus flavor. It is often served on a salad or placed on a cheeseboard next to Bijou, which is the same cheese aged for one month.

Goat Milk Cheese—Aged

Bonne Bouche

A cheese reminiscent of the Loire Valley region of France, Bonne Bouche means "good mouthful" and is indeed a tasty bite. The curd for this cheese is carefully hand ladled, lightly sprinkled with ash, and aged just long enough to develop a rind. After seven to ten days, the cheeses are packaged in their individual crates where they age up to eight weeks. Bonne Bouche, a very creamy cheese, has a fresh, slightly nutty taste. As a young cheese, the rind has a pleasant yeast flavor. As it ages, the cheese becomes softer and the rind becomes more piquant. When Bonne Bouche's rind looks its most dilapidated, and wrinkled is often when it tastes its best.

Bijou

"Bijou" is French for "jewel." This small gem of a cheese has a unique sweet and yeasty flavor. Made according to the traditional French Crottin de Chavignol recipe, Bijou curd coagulates overnight and then is drained in cheese cloth the next day before being shaped into little buttons. First dried, and then ripened for one week, Bijou evolves with time, gaining a sharpness and complexity after thirty days.

Coupole

This American original is named for its likeness to a snow-covered dome shape. Utilizing the same French cheese technology that's involved in making Bijou and Bonne Bouche, Coupole's center has a dense texture and fresh, milky taste. As the cheese ages, the rind develops further, and the aroma becomes stronger on the outside but stays mild on the inside. Coupole's allure is attributable to the intriguing contrast between the strong ripened flavor of the rind and the delicate fresh taste of its interior.

Wine Pairing—Keep It Simple—Trust Your Own Palate

	WHITE	RED
FRESH GOAT CHEESE	Sauvignon Blanc, Pinot Gris, sparkling wine	Rosé de Provence, Barbera, Côte du Rhône
AGED GOAT CHEESE	Cabernet Sauvignon, Australian Riesling	Syrah, light Merlot, Oregon Pinot Noir
WASHED-RIND CHEESE	Gewürztraminer, Riesling, dessert wines	Pinot Noir, Zinfandel
SEMI-HARD TO HARD CHEESE	Gewürztraminer, Riesling, Chardonnay	Cabernet Sauvignon, Merlot, Port
BLUE CHEESE	Riesling, Orange Muscat, dessert wines	Sherry, Zinfandel, Merlot, Dolcetto

Sparkling and whites pair easily and relatively risk-free with all kinds of cheese. The more complex the wine, the more obscure the perfect cheese pairing. The discovery requires an open mind and lots of practice.

Pairing Beyond Beverages

Pairing cheese with different accompaniments is fun and sometimes surprising. Today, American cheese shop counters are filled with all kinds of chutney, fig paste, nuts, dried fruits, specialty breads, crackers, and charcuterie. Here are some ideas:

❯ Goat cheese with dried apricots or fig spread, crostini

❯ Washed-rind cheese with quince paste, white country bread

❯ Hard cheese with apple chutney, dry sausage, plain crackers

❯ Blue cheese with honey or dark chocolate, bread with raisins and nuts

Cheeseboard 101

How much per person?

Tasting plate: ¾ to 1 ounce

Appetizer plate: 1 to 1½ ounces

Main course plate: 1½ ounces

How to taste cheese?

Observe and note the following:

The external appearance: wrinkly, smooth, silky, waxy, hard rind, bandaged...

The interior texture: buttery, dense, creamy, soft, porous, perforated...

The smell: floral, fruity, fresh milk, earthy...

The flavor: sweet, nutty, tangy, grassy, full bodied...

What kind of cheese?

To create a good cheeseboard, go for a variety of textures, shapes, and colors, from a variety of animals (cows, goats, sheep, even water buffalo). For example, here is an American artisanal cheeseboard:

Fresh goat cheese:
Fresh Crottin, Vermont Chèvre

Surface-ripened goat cheese:
Bijou, Bonne Bouche, Coupole, Camillia

Soft-ripened sheep cheese:
La Fleurie, Hudson Valley Camembert

Washed-rind cow cheese:
Blanca Bianca, Grayson, Valfino

Hard cow cheese:
Pleasant Ridge Reserve, Aged Vermont Cheddar, Surchoix Gruyère

Blue cow cheese:
Crater Lake Blue, Gore-Dawn-Zola, Bayley Hazen

Appetizers

CORDIAL CONVERSATION, CHÈVRE AND CANAPÉS CAN CREATE CONNECTION.

My mother-in-law, Marion Hooper, had a hand-painted sign hanging in her kitchen in Mystic, Connecticut, admonishing: "The main thing is not to get panicky." I would add: especially over appetizers.

Appetizers should set a relaxed mood for the evening. Like candles, cordials, and some bluesy jazz in the background, appetizers tell my guests they are special and to enjoy themselves, whether it is a big gathering at a summer barbecue or an intimate winter dinner with a few friends.

Appetizers shouldn't be more than a nibble, just a little something to stave off hunger as guests take in the big smells wafting from the kitchen or grill. Some of my favorite standbys are crème fraîche on smoked salmon,

spinach and mascarpone dip, or goat cheese crostini. The appetizer menu always includes a simple cheese display. Unlike a cheeseboard that you may offer up as a smart finale to a festive meal, the appetizer display doesn't require a large offering of different kinds of cheese. Pick two or three and add some dried fruit, olives, or roasted nuts, and place them on a simple platter or rustic cutting board. Fresh or aged goat cheese is a staple in my "art-of-entertaining" portfolio. It is light and can be perfectly paired with many different drinks and cocktails.

The main thing is not to get panicky. Relax. Imbibe. Laugh. Chat. Connect. My favorite entertaining is the spontaneous gathering of friends at the picnic table in summer, or when people stop by on a cold winter night to enjoy a warm fire and some impromptu but delicious food.

Goat Cheese Crostini with Grilled Vegetables

MAKES > 16 to 20 crostini

INGREDIENTS:

1 baguette, sliced diagonally, ½-inch-thick
½ cup olive oil
Salt and pepper
1 mini-eggplant sliced
½ pound asparagus, blanched and bottoms trimmed
8 mushrooms whole
1 bell pepper cut in half
4 ounces creamy goat cheese, plain
4 ounces creamy goat cheese with olives and herbs
4 ounces creamy goat cheese with roasted red pepper
1 ear of corn in the husk, soaked in water for 15 minutes
¼ cup mixed chopped herbs (thyme, basil, oregano)

DIRECTIONS:

> In a bowl toss sliced bread with 4 tablespoons of olive oil, sprinkle with salt and pepper. Grill bread for 2 to 3 minutes on each side until lightly toasted and grill marks appear. Place bread on a large platter.

> Place the corn on the grill and turn while preparing the other veggies. Corn will grill about 15 minutes.

> Toss veggies with remaining olive oil, sprinkle with salt and pepper, and grill for 3 to 5 minutes on each side until they become soft and show nice grill marks. Set aside to cool to room temperature.

> Slice the eggplant, mushroom, and bell pepper in thin slices or cubes. Slice the asparagus diagonally in 2-inch pieces. Remove the husk from corn and cut off the cob.

> Spread creamy goat cheeses on the bread, top with grilled veggies, and garnish with fresh herbs.

ALTERNATIVE:

> This recipe can also be made in the oven. Toast bread slices on a sheet pan in the oven. Slice all veggies, toss in ¼ cup of olive oil, sprinkle with salt and pepper. Preheat the oven to 425°F and roast for 25 to 30 minutes until veggies are tender.

> If corn is out of season, substitute with one large sweet potato.

Storing Cheese

Cheese has personality, character, and some backbone so treat it with respect but don't baby it.

> The goal is to serve it at its best, which means room temperature for a full and tasty experience. Remove it from the fridge one hour before serving.

> If you are lucky enough to have some left over, rewrap it to keep it from drying out. If the rind feels dry to the touch, wrap in it plastic. If the cheese surface seems too moist and sticky, wrap it loosely in wax paper or leave it open on a plate.

> Cheese will last a long time in your fridge, especially in a drawer away from other foods.

> Most important, eat cheese when you are hungry and crave something satisfying. It is not just for a cheeseboard and recipes.

Warm Spinach Mascarpone Dip

INGREDIENTS:

1 small onion, minced
2 tablespoons olive oil
16 ounces frozen chopped spinach*
8 ounces mascarpone
½ teaspoon salt
½ teaspoon pepper
¼ teaspoon cayenne pepper
½ cup grated Parmesan cheese

*Spinach is first up in the garden in Vermont. All June
 we eat spinach salads. Catch it before it bolts, blanch
 and freeze for a healthy green vegetable all winter long.

DIRECTIONS:

› Preheat oven to 350°F.

› In a large sauté pan over medium heat, cook the onion
  with olive oil until translucent.

› Add frozen spinach and heat until spinach is hot but still
  green. Add mascarpone, salt, pepper, cayenne, Parmesan
  cheese and stir. Pour the mixture into a small casserole or
  baking dish.

› Bake for 30 minutes until bubbling around the edges.
  Serve warm with pita chips or a sliced baguette.

One Dip, Many Recipes

For a quick pizza topped with bacon, spread this dip on
flatbread. It also can be used as the sauce added to cooked
arborio rice for the perfect Italian risotto. Or, stuff a chicken
breast with the leftover dip and bake in the oven until the
meat is cooked.

Chef Raymond Ost

SANDRINE'S BISTRO, CAMBRIDGE, MASSACHUSETTS

Raymond Ost, Sandrine's

Chef Raymond Ost prepares meals at what is described as "the most elegant bistro imaginable." This lovely dining spot, however, is not in Paris or Lyon; it is in the heart of Cambridge, Massachusetts. Sandrine's, named after Raymond's daughter, has a warm Alsatian decor that welcomes diners into a relaxing atmosphere and offers them a cuisine full of robust flavors.

Born in Strasbourg in the Alsace region of France, Raymond began cooking in his teens and then earned a degree from the Ecole Hôtelière. Throughout his career, which spans more than thirty-five years, Raymond has worked as a chef in kitchens from Martinique to Abu Dhabi to San Francisco. He was recently awarded the highest honor given to French chefs, the Maître Ouvrier de France.

On Sandrine's menu, signature dishes like choucroute, a hearty pork and sauerkraut dish typical of Alsace, and kugelhof, a warm chocolate Bundt cake, share prime time with French bistro classics like escargot and bouillabaisse, and with modern recipes like duck breast, or weekly vegetarian and pasta specialties. As one reviewer notes, "Sandrine's menu, produced from an open kitchen, reflects both Raymond's culinary imagination as well as the traditional French bistro reliance on local ingredients."

Raymond's specialty, tarte flambée (or flammekueche in German), goes back almost four hundred years, when French peasants and village bakers pooled their culinary resources. At the end of the day, the bakers had dough left over. After working in the fields all day, the peasants would bring their staples — onions, bacon, and fromage blanc — to the baker's shop. He would roll out a thin crust, put the toppings on it, and bake it in the wood-fired oven that was still warm from baking bread all day. It was a simple but hearty meal for hardworking people to share together.

VBC's fromage blanc creates exactly the right base for tarte flambée, according to Raymond. "It isn't greasy or heavy like Swiss cheese or provolone, which leaves fat on the top of the crust." The fromage blanc has a silky smoothness, which is an excellent contrast to the crispiness of the crust, and the mild flavor of the cheese balances perfectly with the strong taste of the bacon and onion.

Chef Raymond Ost—Sandrine's Bistro, Cambridge, Massachusetts

Flammekueche "French *Tarte Flambée*"

SERVES > 8

DOUGH INGREDIENTS:

2½ cups all-purpose flour

1 cup cold water

¼ teaspoon salt

1 tablespoon instant dry yeast

Makes approximately two, 10-inch free-form
    flammekueche

TOPPING INGREDIENTS:

8 ounces fromage blanc

4 ounces crème fraîche

⅓ cup heavy cream

Pinch of nutmeg

Pinch of white pepper

Pinch of salt

1 tablespoon vegetable oil

1 egg yolk

1½ cups thinly sliced caramelized onions

12 slices hickory-smoked bacon

In a large bowl, whisk together the first 8 ingredients.
Reserve the onions and bacon in separate bowls.

DOUGH DIRECTIONS:

> Line 2 cookie sheets with parchment paper.

> In the bowl of a large mixer, combine all the ingredients.
Mix with a dough hook for 5 to 7 minutes, scraping the
bowl occasionally until the dough forms a sticky ball on the
end of the hook. Transfer the dough to a greased bowl and
cover it with plastic wrap. Let the dough rise in a warm
place until doubled, approximately 1 hour. Punch down and
divide into 2 equal pieces.

> Place 1 piece of dough on a floured board and coat with
flour. With a floured rolling pin, roll out the dough into a
rough rectangle, approximately 10 to 12 inches across and
⅛ inch thick, making sure there is flour on both sides of the
dough at all times. Place dough on a parchment-lined cookie
sheet. Repeat with remaining dough. Cover and refrigerate
any rolled-out dough while you prepare the topping. The
dough can be prepared 1 day in advance, wrapped, and
refrigerated until ready to roll.

ASSEMBLY:

> Preheat oven to 500°F.

> Depending on your oven size, you can cook 2 pans at once, but
adjust racks so that they are close to the bottom of the oven.

> Spread ½ cup of the topping mixture on 1 piece of rolled
dough. Sprinkle with the onions and then the bacon. Repeat
with another sheet of dough. Slide the cookie sheets onto
the lowered racks in the preheated oven. Bake until brown
and crisp, approximately 10 minutes, reversing the sheets
midway through baking to make sure they brown evenly.
Cut into squares and serve immediately.

Crudité Platter with Three Dipping Sauces

PLATTER INGREDIENTS:

2 pounds asparagus, ends cut off
2 tablespoons olive oil
1 tablespoon lemon zest
Salt and pepper to taste
Crudités: carrots, broccoli, cauliflower

TARRAGON DIP INGREDIENTS:

8 ounces quark
1 tablespoon fresh tarragon, chopped
1 tablespoon white or champagne vinegar
1 tablespoon Dijon mustard
1 tablespoon lemon zest
Salt and pepper to taste

ANCHO CHILI DIP INGREDIENTS:

8 ounces mascarpone
2 tablespoons cilantro, chopped
1 chipotle pepper in adobo sauce, chopped fine,
   or 1 teaspoon ancho chili powder
1 tablespoon lime juice
1 teaspoon molasses

GREEK DIP INGREDIENTS*:

8 ounces fromage blanc
1 tablespoon fresh dill or mint, chopped
1 clove garlic, smashed and minced
¼ teaspoon fresh ground pepper
¼ teaspoon sea salt
1 small cucumber, peeled, seeded, and chopped

*This is also the dressing on our Greek Salad.

PLATTER DIRECTIONS:

> Blanch asparagus in boiling water for just 1 minute and then shock in cold water. Dry with a paper towel and put in a bowl and toss with 2 tablespoons of olive oil, lemon zest, and salt and pepper. Preheat grill to medium. Place asparagus on the grill and turn every 2 minutes until done on all sides. This should take about 6 minutes. Serve with other vegetables on a platter with dipping sauce.

DIP DIRECTIONS:

> For each dip, put all ingredients in the food processor and pulse until mixed well. The sauces can be made ahead and kept in the refrigerator for 3 days, if needed.

Veggies at the BBQ

With summer vegetables and fresh herbs in the garden, this is a great barbecue appetizer. The quark dipping sauce also makes a great sauce for hot or cold grilled salmon. Use fromage blanc in this recipe if you desire even less fat.

Cheese Party Gems

CHÈVRE BALLS INGREDIENTS:

8 ounces chèvre, plain

Toppings:

> SPICY: 1/3 cup dried hot peppers (ancho chilies are the best)

> SOPHISTICATED: 1/4 cup chopped fresh lavender and 1/8 cup coarse ground peppercorn

> SWEET: 1/3 cup chopped dried apricots and 1/3 cup candied or spiced pecans or walnuts

BACON-WRAPPED BIJOU INGREDIENTS:

5 Bijou

10 slices high-quality bacon

CHEESE SHOT GLASSES INGREDIENTS:

one 8-ounce jar fresh pesto

one 15-ounce can high-quality roasted red pepper soup, chilled

4 ounces chèvre, plain

3/4 cup pine nuts, toasted

SMOKED SALMON AND CRÈME FRAÎCHE CANAPÉS INGREDIENTS:

8 ounces crème fraîche, whipped until medium peaks form. (This is just like whipping cream, but keep an eye on it because it is quick!)

1 tablespoon fresh or pickled horseradish, chopped fine

1 tablespoon chives, minced

1 teaspoon lemon peel, grated

Salt and freshly ground pepper to taste

12 slices of 1- x 1-inch Danish pumpernickel bread

6 ounces smoked salmon, thinly sliced

1 tablespoon dill, chopped

CHÈVRE BALLS DIRECTIONS:

> Cut each chèvre log into 12 pieces and roll into a small ball (most easily done when chèvre is at room temperature). Roll ball in topping and place on a plate and serve. These can be made a day in advance and refrigerated. Bring up to room temperature before serving.

BACON-WRAPPED BIJOU DIRECTIONS:

> Wrap each Bijou with 2 slices of bacon, crosswise. Bake in the oven at 400°F for 10 minutes, until bacon is cooked. Blot baked-oil bacon fat with paper towel, let cool for 5 minutes before serving.

CHEESE SHOT GLASSES DIRECTIONS:

> Use eight 2½ to 3 ounce shot glasses. For each glass, pour 2 tablespoons of pesto, then 2 tablespoons of soup, then crumble some chèvre on top, and add 1 tablespoon of pine nuts.

SMOKED SALMON AND CRÈME FRAÎCHE CANAPÉS DIRECTIONS:

> Mix crème fraîche, horseradish, chives, and lemon peel in a small bowl. Add salt and pepper. Spread 1 teaspoon of the mixture over each bread slice. Divide smoked salmon among bread slices. Sprinkle each canapé with dill.

Soups & Salads

TOO OFTEN RELEGATED, THESE SUPPORTING ACTORS
ARE CAPABLE OF STEALING THE SHOW.

On one of our junkets, um, I mean important research expeditions to France, Bob and I made a point of ordering the *salade de chèvre chaud* that is a staple on every bistro menu. Shaped like a pillbox, the little Crottin de Chavignol is placed on a slice of baguette with the rind facing up and then put under the broiler until it starts to caramelize. Finally, it lands on a bed of fresh green lettuce with a simple vinaigrette. It's impeccable.

On a visit to Greece with our spouses, Bob and I discovered Greek yogurt and "real" old-country feta cheese made from a blend of goat and sheep milk. Workaday Greek salad was nothing more than a slab of feta atop a plate of fresh lettuce blessed with Kalamata olives and tomatoes. Once back home, living vicariously, we developed the kind of feta we fell in love with in Greece. We also incorporated this simple nourishing salad into our own repertoire and even created our own variation with spinach and fromage blanc cucumber dressing. It has become a perfect lunch to have under a big maple tree on a hot summer day.

During the long, cold Vermont winter, I make soups to give my family a hot, comforting school lunch or quick, nourishing supper after an afternoon of pond hockey. Whether I am cooking butternut squash soup in my mother's old Dutch oven, a simple corn chowder, or minestrone, there is always the crème fraîche on the counter to spoon in as a finishing touch.

Warm Toasted Bijou Salad

INGREDIENTS:

4 leeks, the white and light-green section only,
　　cut in half lengthwise and washed
½ cup olive oil
Salt and freshly ground pepper
1 tablespoon Dijon mustard
3 tablespoons balsamic vinegar
4 Bijou, cut in half horizontally
8 slices French baguette, ¾ inch thick
1 head romaine lettuce, trimmed, washed, and spun
1 cup cherry tomatoes, cut in half

DIRECTIONS:

⟩ Pat dry and toss leeks with a splash of olive oil and season with salt and pepper. Broil in the oven for about 5 minutes until tender but not mushy! Let the leeks cool, then chop thinly and put in a medium-size bowl.

⟩ Prepare the dressing. Mix together the mustard, vinegar, olive oil, and leeks, and let sit for 4 hours to 1 week.

⟩ Put a medallion of the Bijou, rind facing up, on each baguette slice and place under the broiler until the cheese is soft to a little runny. The rind should be slightly golden (about 2 to 3 minutes).

⟩ Serve immediately over mixed greens tossed in the leek vinaigrette and the tomatoes.

Marinated Bijou

In Provence, France, every home cook has a little jar of homemade marinated goat cheese on his or her counter. This little jar usually contains a combination of the region's best products: one or two Picodon (an aged goat cheese similar in taste to our Bijou), sprigs of lavender, herbes de Provence, and possibly garlic. These simple ingredients are preserved in the local extra virgin olive oil.

It is easy to prepare and makes a great Provençale gift with a unique Vermont twist.

Chef Eric Ripert

LE BERNARDIN, NEW YORK, NEW YORK

The difference between a "chef" and a "cook," says Eric Ripert, executive chef at Le Bernardin in New York City, is that a chef is a title, a cook "is who you are. . . . it's your spine and your soul." The cook Eric was to become began in his family's kitchen. "I was probably the only guy allowed in the kitchen," Eric remembers. "I ate everything all the time." When his family moved from Antibes, on the coast of France, to Andorra, just over the Spanish border, the Mediterranean cuisine mingled with the rich saffron flavors of the Pyrenees.

In 1991, after working at some of the most prestigious restaurants in Paris and New York, Eric was recruited by Gilbert Le Coze and his sister Maguy to be chef for Le Bernardin. Three years later, however, Le Coze had a fatal heart attack. At 29, Eric stepped into Le Coze's shoes. "I was naive. I wasn't out in the world. I didn't hear people doubting my capabilities," Eric notes. The following year, Ripert's Le Bernardin was awarded the maximum four stars from the *New York Times*. While remaining true to Le Coze's philosophy of only the freshest fish in light sauces, Eric has put his own signature on the menu — seafood delicately infused with unusual herbs and spices, marinades of cilantro, mint, and jalapeños. He has also added a bit of

environmental consciousness to the menu, alerting his patrons that the restaurant supports the Natural Resources Defense Council and SeaWeb's educational efforts to speed the recovery of endangered species, and so will not serve fish that fall under this category.

Although soft cheeses are not paired with fish, "fish love butter," he says. "But because fish is very subtle, you can't have a sauce that is too rich — the right balance of butter and cream is critical: crème fraîche, yes; fish risotto with mascarpone; and, of course, poached fish in butter and milk."

When Eric does use cheese, he leans strongly toward goat cheese. "It has a strong personality," he notes, "a lot of sweetness and a little bit of pepper." Eric's goat cheese "parfait" salad is slightly tart and tangy, which the crème fraîche balances with some sweetness. The rich blend of sweet potatoes and apples does not mask the cheese, he says, but "announces it." The Mediterranean touch of black olives adds richness and a little saltiness to the cheese. This is a dish that brings fine dining to your table.

Chef Eric Ripert — Le Bernardin, New York, New York

Goat Cheese Parfait

SERVES > 6

PARFAIT INGREDIENTS:

3 medium apples
2 sweet potatoes (about 1½ pounds)
Fine sea salt
Freshly ground white pepper
3 tablespoon olive oil
10 ounces chèvre, plain
6 ounces crème fraîche
1 small shallot, minced (about 1 tablespoon)
1 tablespoon chives, sliced

CRÈME FRAÎCHE SAUCE INGREDIENTS:

4 ounces crème fraîche
1 tablespoon shallots, minced
1 tablespoon parsley, chopped
1 tablespoon chives, sliced
2 teaspoons lemon juice
Fine sea salt and freshly ground pepper

SALAD INGREDIENTS:

1 cup celery leaves
2 tablespoons black olives, diced
1 tablespoon lemon, diced
1 tablespoon lemon juice
2 tablespoons lemon oil
Salt and freshly ground pepper
¼ cup celery, sliced on a bias about ¼ inch long

SPECIAL EQUIPMENT:

6 ring molds — 2 inches in diameter by 3 inches high

DIRECTIONS:

› Preheat oven to 400°F.

› Season the apples and sweet potatoes with salt and pepper and drizzle with olive oil. Individually wrap the sweet potatoes and apples in aluminum foil, and place them in the preheated oven. The apples will be tender in about 20 minutes, and the sweet potatoes will need about 35 to 40 minutes of cooking time. Once they are tender, remove them from the foil.

› When the apples and sweet potatoes are cool enough to handle, peel and dice into ¼-inch pieces. Reserve.

› While the apples and sweet potatoes are cooling, combine the parfait ingredients, the chèvre and crème fraîche, in a bowl and mix completely. Stir in the shallot and chives. Season to taste with salt and pepper. Reserve in the refrigerator.

› For the crème fraîche sauce, mix the crème fraîche, shallots, parsley, chives, and lemon juice in a stainless-steel mixing bowl. Season with salt and pepper.

› Before serving, remove the chèvre mixture from the refrigerator and bring to room temperature.

› Place a ring mold in the center of each plate and spread 1 tablespoon of the chèvre mixture in the bottom. Top the chèvre with the diced sweet potato, then add another dollop of chèvre, then the diced apple, another dollop of chèvre, then the diced sweet potato. Finish with a layer of chèvre.

› Toss the celery leaves, slices of celery, black olives, and lemon together. Drizzle with lemon juice and lemon oil and season with salt and pepper. Top each parfait with a bit of the celery salad, and then remove the mold. Place the parfait in the middle of a plate and drizzle the crème fraîche sauce around the plate and decorate with celery. Serve immediately.

Greek-Style Feta and Spinach Salad
with Cucumber Dressing

SALAD INGREDIENTS:

one 8-ounce bag of baby spinach, washed and dried
1 pint of mixed red and yellow cherry tomatoes,
   cut in half
1 small red onion, sliced thin
4 ounces of Kalamata olives
4 ounces feta

DRESSING INGREDIENTS:

8 ounces fromage blanc
1 tablespoon fresh mint, chopped
1 clove garlic, smashed and minced
¼ teaspoon freshly ground peppercorn
¼ teaspoon sea salt
1 small cucumber, peeled, seeded, and chopped

DIRECTIONS:

› Put all the dressing ingredients in a food processor and
pulse until mixed well. This can be made ahead and kept
for 3 days if needed.

› Toss salad ingredients with dressing and top with feta
triangles, cubes, or slices.

Milk Begets Cheese

In Vermont, the average cow produces a little less than
20,000 pounds of milk per year. That's about 10,000 quarts
per cow, enough to fill a typical family fridge 33 times over
the course of a year. Goats produce about one-tenth what
cows produce. It takes about 10 pounds of either cow or goat
milk to make a pound of hard or aged cheese. Fresh chèvre
can be made with less milk, about six pounds.

Summer Mango and Tomato Gazpacho
with Lime Fromage Blanc Sorbet

GAZPACHO INGREDIENTS:

1 cup cold water

1 cup tomato juice

8 large tomatoes, peeled, seeded, and diced

1 large mango, peeled, seeded, and diced

¼ cup red onion, minced

1 clove garlic, minced

1 cucumber, peeled and diced

1 green bell pepper, seeded and minced

4 scallions, chopped fine

1 orange, juiced (zest set aside for the sorbet)

¼ cup fresh lime juice

¼ cup cilantro, chopped

1 teaspoon salt

1 teaspoon freshly ground pepper

½ teaspoon cayenne pepper

Add 2 teaspoons sugar if the mango and tomato
  are not quite ripe.

SORBET INGREDIENTS:

8 ounces fromage blanc

⅛ cup fresh lime juice

1 tablespoon orange zest

Zest of 1 lime

1 teaspoon sugar

GAZPACHO DIRECTIONS:

› Place all ingredients except the orange zest in a large
  bowl or container overnight. Adjust seasonings in the
  morning. If the mixture is too chunky, pulse half of it with
  a hand mixer.

SORBET DIRECTIONS:

› Mix all ingredients together in a bowl and put in freezer
  2 hours before serving. Use a small melon baller or sorbet
  scoop. Place sorbet on top of gazpacho.

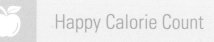

Happy Calorie Count

This fat-free dairy sorbet will satisfy any sweet tooth.
Fromage blanc is made with skim milk, has a high protein
content, and is low in salt. Our sorbet recipe refreshes savory
summer dishes, such as gazpacho and other cold soups.
To cookies or warm comfort desserts like cobblers, the sorbet
adds few calories and no guilt!

Winter Crème Fraîche Baked Potato Soup

INGREDIENTS:

5 baked potatoes
4 slices of bacon, chopped
1 small onion, diced
⅓ cup all-purpose flour
6 cups 1% milk
1 cup sharp cheddar cheese, shredded
8 ounces crème fraîche
1 teaspoon ground black pepper
¾ cup scallions, chopped

DIRECTIONS:

› In the oven, bake the potatoes at 400°F for one hour, then peel and mash coarsely.

› In a large casserole, cook the bacon and onions over medium heat until onions are translucent.

› Sprinkle the flour over the onions and bacon and stir until the mixture starts to bubble.

› Lower the heat and gradually whisk in the milk until blended. Turn heat back to medium and allow the milk mixture to thicken and come to a slow boil while stirring.

› Add mashed potatoes and cheese stirring until the cheese is melted.

› Lower the heat and add the crème fraîche, black pepper, and half of the scallions. Cook over low heat for about 10 minutes, until hot (do not boil).

› Place soup in 8 bowls and garnish with remaining scallions and more grated cheese if you like.

 Crème Fraîche Delight

Compared to sour cream, crème fraîche has a higher butterfat content (42% versus 18%). Fat adds a lot of flavor. It is cultured, which makes it slightly acidic. This acidity gives the cream stability when mixed with wine, lemon, or other acidic ingredients and prevents it from separating when heated. According to Steve Jenkins, cheese buyer for Fairway Markets, "It's one of the most extraordinary substances in the world of dairy, of gastronomy. To compare it to American sour cream is to compare spam to foie gras."

Everyday Fare

EXPAND YOUR REPETOIRE; ELEGANT, MAYBE DECEPTIVE. ZERO TO SIXTY IN TWENTY MINUTES.

Most of us are too busy to plan and then execute fancy meals every day. If the ingredients are simple and at hand, that is a bonus. The recipes here are for everyday, and are quick and easy. My mother's everyday, surefire fallback fare was elegant deception: cheese soufflé. Such a treat. Little did we know that it was actually just a few eggs and some decent cheese. In those days, the fridge always harbored a modest stash of Vermont cheddar for the soufflé. My mother's prestidigitation dazzled me as she built beautiful, but seemingly undoable, magical mountains of browned egg whites. Years later, I discovered how embarrassingly simple a soufflé is to make and what goat cheese adds for an amazing new flavor. Right there in your fridge are all the ingredients.

Mom also made a winning, no-frills Quiche Lorraine with good ham and gruyère. Sometimes she would embellish it with spinach, mustard, or bacon. Today, we make it sing by adding goat cheese, sun-dried tomatoes, or portobello mushrooms. The crust is the only remotely hard part. This no-fat, crustless fromage blanc and leek quiche is guilt-free simplicity, compliments of Mireille Guiliano, author of *French Women Don't Get Fat*. We admonish you to take pleasure in preparing your meals. Alison Lane and Andrew Silva, the chefs/owners of Mirabelles in Burlington, Vermont, have two wonderful savory everyday dishes — smoked salmon scones and a spinach and mushroom panini. Theirs is just the kind of food that we crave for our daily meals. Though quick and easy to prepare, take Mireille's advice and enjoy it slowly.

Chefs Alison Lane & Andrew Silva

MIRABELLES, BURLINGTON, VERMONT

Tamales and tea cakes, Andrew Silva and Alison Lane come from different cooking backgrounds. In Texas, Andrew cooked as a hobby. "It took a few years, and plenty of people pushing me, to decide to go to cooking school," explains Andrew. Alison's British mother was a plain cook, but loved making desserts and ran a tea room in North Carolina. When her parents moved to Vermont, Alison, who already had a degree in business management, decided it would be a kick to go to culinary school. Eventually, the two future business partners met at the New England Culinary Institute in Montpelier, Vermont.

After internships at restaurants and pastry shops in England, France, and California, and teaching at NECI's Essex, Vermont, campus, they decided if they were going to work that hard, they should work for themselves. Coming from a family of entrepreneurs, Alison never really thought about it. "Let's do it," she remembers thinking, "and Andrew is so good-natured he willingly signed his life away."

Walking into Mirabelles today, you are immediately wrapped in the warm, delicious smells of freshly baked pastries, cakes, and other tantalizing morsels. In 1990, when Alison and Andrew opened their shop, there was nothing like this European-style bakery in Burlington, Vermont. Along with their vision of a comfortable place where people could enjoy French-inspired pastries and a good cup of coffee was their policy of buying local ingredients whenever possible. "It wasn't something that we really thought about consciously — it was a given. It was good food, and it was here," explains Alison. "We've been using Vermont Butter & Cheese products for more than seventeen years."

A few years ago, they expanded the dining area, and the cafe quickly became a favorite spot for meals, dessert, or coffee. And now the denizens of this small city along Lake Champlain are sure to find delicious, creative, freshly prepared entrees for breakfast and lunch. Among their frequent offerings are two dishes we've included. Alison's recipe for "Chèvre and Smoked Salmon Scones" is a wonderful combination of slightly salty smoked salmon and the tang of goat cheese that ripples through the soft, savory bread. Andrew also uses goat cheese in his "Spinach and Mushroom Panini," which absorbs the rich flavors of the portobello mushrooms, capers, olives, and spinach. He says he loves using creamy goat cheese because it is so versatile — add it to salads, spread it on sandwiches, or pipe it through a bag for decoration.

BRUNCH AT MIRABELLES

Alison's Chèvre and Smoked Salmon Scones

MAKES > 10

INGREDIENTS:

2 cups all-purpose flour
1 tablespoon baking powder
1 teaspoon kosher salt
4 ounces cultured butter unsalted, cubed
5 ounces chèvre, plain, crumbled
3 ounces smoked salmon, chopped
3 tablespoons chives, chopped
¾ cup half-and-half

DIRECTIONS:

> Preheat oven to 400°F.

> Combine flour, baking powder, salt, and butter in a bowl and cut in the butter with a pastry cutter until the butter is the size of peas. Add crumbled chèvre and mix just to evenly distribute the cheese. Add salmon and chives and mix.

> Pour the half-and-half in all at once and mix until it just combines. Dump onto a floured surface, pat into a rectangle, and cut into triangles.

> Place on a parchment-lined sheet pan and brush with egg wash.

> Bake for about 20 minutes, until brown.

BRUNCH AT MIRABELLES

Andrew's Spinach and Mushroom Panini

SERVES 〉 4

INGREDIENTS:

1 sweet red bell pepper
2 portobello mushrooms
3 tablespoons olive oil
2 tablespoons thyme, chopped
1 teaspoon rosemary, chopped
1 garlic clove, minced fine
Salt and freshly ground pepper
8 ounces creamy goat cheese, plain
2 tablespoons imported green olives, chopped
1 tablespoon capers, rinsed and chopped
8 slices sourdough or country bread
1 cup loose baby spinach

DIRECTIONS:

〉 Char the red pepper over a flame or under the broiler until blackened. Place in a covered bowl to steam for 5 minutes. Remove char and stem from pepper and slice into ¼-inch strips.

〉 Steam and scrape out the gills of mushrooms with a spoon, cut in half and slice into ¼-inch slices. Heat olive oil over medium heat. Add mushrooms and sauté until wilted and tender. Add the thyme, rosemary, and garlic, and season with salt and pepper. Remove from heat and allow to cool. In a bowl, combine goat cheese, mushroom mixture, roasted red pepper, olives, and capers.

〉 Spread the goat cheese mixture on one side of the bread and top with a handful of spinach and another slice of bread. Brush with additional olive oil and cook in a panini grill or in a heavy-bottomed sauté pan until golden. Turn once if cooking in a sauté pan. Cut in half or in quarters.

Goat Cheese Mini-Soufflés

THE SOUFFLÉS INGREDIENTS:

3 ounces cultured butter lightly salted
2 tablespoons bread crumbs
2 ounces all-purpose flour
8 ounces whole milk
16 ounces chèvre, plain
6 eggs, separated
1 dash Tabasco
Salt and ground black pepper to taste

SALAD INGREDIENTS:

¾ pound arugula
1 cup candied walnuts
1 cup pink grapefruit

CHAMPAGNE VINAIGRETTE INGREDIENTS:

6 tablespoons champagne vinegar
3 teaspoons salt
1½ teaspoons freshly ground pepper
¾ cup olive oil

DIRECTIONS:

⟩ Preheat oven to 350°F.

⟩ Rub the inside of six ¾-cup soufflé dishes or two and a half muffin tins with 1 ounce of butter. Coat with bread crumbs, and tap out excess. Set aside.

⟩ Lightly toast flour in a heavy-bottomed pot over medium heat. Add butter and stir until flour and butter are combined to form a roux. Add milk while whisking over medium heat. Whisk until smooth and roux thickens to a smooth mashed-potato consistency.

⟩ Remove from heat and allow to cool. Add chèvre and egg yolks and mix using a rubber spatula, until well combined. Season the base with Tabasco, salt, and pepper.

⟩ While base is cooling, whip egg whites until they form soft peaks, then fold into soufflé base.

⟩ Divide the mixture among prepared soufflé dishes. Bake in the oven until they puff and are golden brown (about 50 minutes).

⟩ Whisk together vinegar, salt, and pepper in a large bowl, then add the oil in a slow stream, whisking until emulsified.

⟩ Prepare the salad by dividing the arugula onto 6 plates. Top with candied walnuts and grapefruit, and drizzle with 2 tablespoons of champagne vinaigrette.

⟩ Once baked, remove soufflés from the oven. If they fall, this is all right. Cool and run a small sharp knife around the sides of the dishes to loosen the soufflés. Serve immediately on the salad.

Author Mireille Guiliano

FRENCH WOMEN DON'T GET FAT, UNITED STATES AND FRANCE

Why are most French women slender? Mireille Guiliano, former CEO of Clicquot Inc. (the U.S. subsidiary of Champagne Veuve Clicquot) and devoted food lover, gives us several reasons in her books *French Women Don't Get Fat* and *French Women for All Seasons*. The French in general do not eat "on the run" or while doing something else like working at a desk in front of a computer. Rather, a meal is an event that is to be enjoyed slowly, with all of one's senses engaged. When you eat deliberately, you eat less. Unfortunately, Americans multitask 24/7. Mireille, who lives in the United States part of the year with her American husband, knows our ways only too well. "It is very easy to eat in front of a computer at work," she says, "but what do we gain? We eat more poorly. We eat more. We eat without pleasure."

Two other approaches to staying in shape are moderation and variety. Instead of great mounds of steak and potatoes with gravy, a French meal may consist of small portions of meat or fish, fresh vegetables, or maybe just a soup accompanied by some cheese and bread. French pastries are legendary, but the French don't gorge themselves on rich bakery goods every day — good bread, yes, croissants, *non merci.* After a main meal at lunch, Mireille and her husband will often have a simple supper, maybe a few sliced tomatoes (when they are in season, *bien sûr*), some fresh goat cheese, a little olive oil, basil,

a piece of bread, a glass of wine, and end with a fruit—*voilà.*

Mireille stresses it is not only the way the French who don't get fat eat, but the quality of food they demand. Along with fresh produce, meat, and fish, good cheese — more often than not locally produced — is an essential part of the French diet.

Mireille's recipe is a wonderful combination of good ingredients and a new twist on a classic dish — quiche. First and foremost are the leeks. When Mireille was a teenager struggling with the weight she had gained in the United States, a doctor prescribed a weekend of eating a special leek broth. She explains that "leeks are a mild diuretic and low in calories, but highly nutritional." The prescription helped her regain her healthier traditional French eating habits and sparked a lifelong love of leeks. In developing her recipe for quiche, she substitutes calories but never for flavor. In addition to the leeks, Mireille uses fromage blanc (cheese), milk instead of cream, and the innovative cabbage "crust," which gives the quiche a lightness that makes it a deliciously lean lunch for a group of friends or an easy evening meal. *Merci madame!*

Author Mirielle Guiliano — *French Women Don't Get Fat*, United States and France

Leeks and Fromage Blanc Quiche

SERVES 〉 6

INGREDIENTS:

1 head savoy cabbage
2 leeks, white parts only, sliced
2 medium onions, peeled and diced
1 tablespoon olive oil
5 ounces spinach, washed and chopped
Salt and freshly ground pepper
2 large eggs
8 ounces fromage blanc
½ cup whole milk
1 cup gruyère cheese, grated
Pinch of nutmeg

DIRECTIONS:

〉 Preheat oven to 350°F.

〉 Discard the outer leaves of the cabbage and blanch the inner leaves until tender, about 10 minutes (the water need not be salted). Put the cooked leaves on paper towels to cool and dry out, then line a nonstick, oven-safe frying pan with the leaves.

〉 Sauté the leeks and onions in the oil over medium heat until tender. Add the spinach. Season with salt and pepper to taste. Continue to cook until the spinach has begun to wilt, then drain the vegetables in a colander.

〉 Blend the eggs, fromage blanc, milk, cheese, and nutmeg, season with salt and pepper to taste, and fold the mixture with the drained vegetables. Carefully pour it into the cabbage-lined pan.

〉 Bake in the preheated oven for 30 minutes or until the quiche is firm to the touch. Allow it to rest for 10 minutes before serving.

 ## The French Way

Make it simple. Quiche is a favorite dish, but we often don't make it because we don't have the time or we think it will be too fattening. Having quiche is not the same as having a thick chocolate brownie: take your favorite quiche recipe, remove the crust, switch the bacon over to ham, the heavy cream to skim-milk fromage blanc, and the cheese to veggies. You will have probably cut out more than half of the calories but added tons of great pleasure. This is one of many tips that French women have up their sleeves, in addition to taking the stairs, walking everywhere, preparing their own meals, and enjoying good food.

Penne Pasta with Garden Tomatoes, Herbs, and Bijou

SERVES > 8

INGREDIENTS:

2 pounds garden tomatoes, chopped
½ cup fresh herbs: basil, thyme, parsley, oregano
    (all or a mix of a few), chopped
4 cloves garlic, crushed
1 teaspoon kosher salt
1 teaspoon freshly ground pepper
1 pound penne pasta
½ cup olive oil
4 Bijou cut in quarters, at room temperature

DIRECTIONS:

> Toss the tomatoes with the herbs, garlic, salt, and pepper in a large bowl and allow to sit at room temperature for 1 hour.

> Bring 6 quarts of salted water to a boil. Stir in the penne and cook until al dente, 8 to 10 minutes, stirring occasionally.

> Drain pasta and return to pan. Add the tomato mixture and olive oil to the penne and stir. Check the seasonings and then gently stir in the quartered Bijou. Cover the pot for 3 minutes, then serve immediately. Bijou will be slightly melted and delicious. Garnish with more freshly ground pepper if needed.

 Go Local

The quality and beauty of Vermont's landscape depend on working farms. The Vermont Fresh Network connects farmers and food producers to restaurants and consumers; a vital link to sustaining our agriculture that also fosters production of high quality food. The Vermont Fresh Network is our partner in connecting talented and thoughtful chefs and consumers with our cheeses.

Main Courses

STARRING CRÈME FRAÎCHE: AMBIDEXTROUS, VIRTUOSO, INCOGNITO.

As a college kid in France, I was exposed to something I call *"la cuisine Française quotidienne"* (daily French cooking). My elderly landlady, Mme de Vulpian, did not eat great quantities, but instead devoted great care and planning to what she would prepare. Her root-cellar-size basement-kitchen always smelled wonderful. I felt privileged to accompany her to her family country home north of Paris. There we prepared a meal together, and I discovered the secret of crème fraîche. Mme de Vulpian seared a simple pork chop on the skillet. Once lightly cooked, she removed the chop from the pan, adding just enough wine to deglaze the pan, then threw in some shallots, prepared mustard, and a heaping tablespoonful of crème fraîche. The creamy sauce simmered and reduced for less than a minute. We added some chopped parsley. Simple, and out of this world.

When I lived on the farm in Brittany, the farm's crème fraîche went into everything. We sautéed green beans and garlic to a light crunch. The crème fraîche glazed the beans and enhanced the *gratin dauphinois* with a nutty flavor. *Tarte Tatin,* a kind of upside-down tart, was topped with dollops of crème fraîche. Our daily portion of fromage blanc was garnished with sugar and crème fraîche for dessert.

As a true French chef, Chef Michel uses crème fraîche in his salmon dish — just a light cream sauce without flour. Chef Dan's pistou is pure and simple. The cheese and crème fraîche add richness, which leaves us feeling satisfied and indulged.

Chef Michel Richard

CITRONELLE AND CENTRAL, WASHINGTON DC

Chef Michel Richard describes his cuisine this way: "Much of my food today is like *trompe l'oeil* (trick of the eye). My food is 'trompe mouth.' Your brain is ready to taste something, but when the food lands in your mouth, you have a different flavor, one you didn't expect!"

From the moment he touched down on U.S. shores from France in the mid-1970s, he was intrigued with American cuisine, subsequently raising it to new heights. On his way from New York to a new job in Santa Fe, New Mexico, with two dollars in his pocket, he had an epicurean epiphany when he stopped and bought some fried chicken. "It was a wonderful discovery to bite into a crispy, crunchy chicken and inside was moist," he remembers. "It was a wonderful surprise because in France we don't have the crunchy textures, we have smooth textures." Coming to call himself, "Captain Crunch," Michel has since shaken the gastronomic world with his technical innovations and his intrepid exploration of flavors and textures. "I want the mouth to dance, to rock 'n' roll — creamy, crunch, a little spice. I want to create happy mouth," Michel explains with a twinkle in his voice.

Michel Richard, Citronelle

And "happy mouth" is exactly what you'll experience at either of Michel's two premier restaurants in Washington DC. At Citronelle, his elegant flagship restaurant, every bite is a witty surprise. "Scrambled eggs" are actually stealthy scallops. A hard-boiled egg is, in reality, mozzarella masquerading as cooked egg white embracing an imposter yolk of yellow tomato gelée. At Central (Citronelle's sister restaurant), everyday fare is turned haute with such conventional dishes as his crispy fried chicken with zesty mustard sauce or the smooth-as-silk, creamy goat cheese Caesar salad.

Michel's recipe for "Cucumber Salmon" brings the unexpected together. The cool, refreshing taste of cucumber cooked in crème fraîche and lightly infused with Dijon mustard and lemon, a combination that heightens the fresh flavor of the fish. The crème fraîche is key. "Without the crème," Michel explains, "it is like eating a hot salad, but with it, you are eating a richer cooked vegetable."

Chef Michel Richard — Citronelle and Central, Washington DC

Crème Fraîche Cucumber Salmon

SERVES > 4

CUCUMBERS INGREDIENTS:

2 cucumbers, peeled, halved lengthwise, seeded, and
    cut crosswise into ¼-inch-wide slices
½ cup clam juice or fish stock
4 ounces crème fraîche
2 egg yolks, at room temperature
1 teaspoon Dijon mustard
2 tablespoons lemon juice, freshly squeezed
2 tablespoons fresh chives or green onions, minced
Salt and freshly ground black pepper to taste

SALMON:

4 salmon fillets (1½ to 2 pounds total), skinned; or
    steaks, ¾ inch thick, patted dry
Salt and freshly ground black pepper to taste
1 ounce cultured butter unsalted
2 tablespoons water

DIRECTIONS:

› For the cucumbers, cook the slices in a heavy medium skillet with the clam juice and crème fraîche over medium–high heat until tender when pierced with a knife, about 5 minutes, stirring occasionally. (This can be prepared ahead, cooled, covered, and set aside at room temperature for up to 2 hours, or refrigerated.)

› To finish the cucumber sauce, in a small bowl whisk the egg yolks, mustard, and lemon juice to blend. Bring the cucumber mixture to a boil. Gradually whisk about ½ cup of the cucumber mixture into the egg yolk mixture, then gradually whisk this mixture back into the cucumbers. Add chives and stir over low heat without boiling until sauce thickens, about 7 minutes. Season with salt and pepper. (This can be prepared several hours ahead and kept warm in a wide-mouthed thermos.)

› For the salmon, season the fish with salt and pepper. Melt the butter in a heavy, large nonstick skillet over medium heat. Turn salmon in butter, add water, cover and simmer until opaque and just cooked through, about 6 to 7 minutes total, turning halfway.

› To serve, ladle cucumber sauce onto 4 plates. Place the salmon in the center of the sauce. Serve immediately.

Lobster Mascarpone Risotto

INGREDIENTS:

6 cups seafood broth or clam juice
2 tablespoons cultured butter with sea salt crystals
1 cup onion, minced
2 cups arborio rice
½ cup dry white wine
4 ounces mascarpone
¼ cup fresh parsley, chopped
Zest of 1 lemon
1½ pounds cooked lobster meat

DIRECTIONS:

› In a large saucepan, bring the broth to a simmer. Cover and keep warm over low heat. Melt the butter in a large casserole over medium heat. Add onion and sauté until tender and translucent, about 5 minutes. Add rice and stir 2 minutes. Add wine and stir until absorbed, about 1 minute. Stir in 1 cup warm broth and simmer until absorbed, stirring frequently. Cook until rice is almost tender, adding broth ½ cup at a time, stirring often and allowing each addition to be absorbed before adding the next, about 20 minutes.

› When cooked, add the mascarpone, half of the parsley, lemon zest, and lobster meat.

› Stir gently and then cover and leave on low heat for about 5 minutes, until seafood is warm and all the liquid has disappeared. Serve in large bowls garnished with the remaining parsley.

Please Share

Occasionally we get ahead of ourselves and have some great cheese in the cooler that has too short a shelf life left to ship! We take it to the Vermont Foodbank. They make it into meals that are sent out to Vermonters who need good food in tough times.

Please, if you're in position where sometimes you have a surplus, make an extra effort to connect to a food shelf, soup kitchen, or shelter. If you have a home vegetable garden, consider planting an extra row to share with those who have less.

www.vtfoodbank.org

Sea Salt Butter Basted Chicken

INGREDIENTS:

4 ounces cultured butter with sea salt crystals, softened
¼ cup mixed herbs (thyme, rosemary, and parsley), chopped
2 cloves garlic, minced
1 teaspoon freshly ground pepper
1 tablespoon lemon zest
1 chicken (3 to 6 pounds)

Compound Butters

The blending of butter with other ingredients, called "compound butter," is a quick and easy way to give your dish a new spin. Make logs of different combinations and freeze them. Then each time you need a little flavor boost, just slice off a medallion of the flavored butter that fits with your dish. Here are some ideas:

Vermont Maple Butter — butter and maple syrup blend for pancakes and waffles

Orange Butter — honey, orange juice and zest, and almonds for crepes

Beurre Maître d'Hotel — parsley, lemon juice and zest, salt, and pepper for steak frites

Blue Butter — crumbled blue cheese, toasted walnuts, and fresh ground black pepper for steaks or burgers

Herb Butter — shallots, rosemary, thyme, salt, and pepper for roasted chicken

Lemon Butter — lemon juice and zest, dill, garlic, salt, and pepper for fish

Truffle Butter — truffle peelings and truffle oil for mashed potatoes and beef

DIRECTIONS:

> Preheat oven to 450°F.

> In a bowl, mix the butter with the herbs and seasonings until incorporated.

> Gently pull away the skin on the chicken and stuff in two-thirds of the butter, then flatten with your hand. Melt the rest of the butter in a pan and brush the outside of the chicken. Baste every 15 to 20 minutes with the juices from the pan. Roast until done, about 50 to 70 minutes.

> For a supermoist, juicy bird, allow the chicken to rest for 15 minutes once it's out of the oven. The juices in the pan make a wonderful butter-rich gravy.

TURKEY ALTERNATIVE:

> For a 14- to 18-pound turkey, soften 8 ounces of cultured butter with sea salt crystals in a bowl. Add ½ cup of fresh herbs (parsley, sage, and thyme) and 1 teaspoon freshly ground pepper. Mix until incorporated, and then follow chicken basting directions. Roast on lower level of the oven at 450°F for 30 minutes, then cover with aluminum foil and reduce the temperature to 350°F. A 14- to 16-pound turkey requires 2 to 2½ hours. Let the turkey rest, loosely covered, for 15 minutes before carving.

Chef Dan Barber

BLUE HILL RESTAURANT, NEW YORK, NEW YORK

Vermont Butter & Cheese's commitment to the agricultural community and to having the quality of its products tied to the land is also a basic tenet for Dan Barber's work. Dan is the Executive Chef/co-owner of the Blue Hill restaurants in New York City and at Stone Barns in Pocantico Hills, New York. Working on his grandmother's farm as a young teenager imbued Dan with a love of the land, a love of food, and, ultimately, a mission to consciously bring the two together in his life as a chef. Dan's hope is that the skill and task of the farmer and the chef become one and the same. "I would love to see the day when you see someone out in a field weeding and harvesting and then that evening you see him or her in the kitchen. I want to blur the line between the overall and the white coat."

Dan ran a catering service for a number of years that specialized in cooking with sustainably grown and locally produced ingredients. Then in 2000, Dan, his brother David, and sister-in-law Laureen opened a small restaurant in a former speakeasy in New York City's East Village. The Blue Hill restaurant, named after their grandmother's farm, grew from a noted neighborhood restaurant to one of national acclaim. The family stayed true to their ties to the land by buying as much locally grown food as possible and keeping their menu seasonal.

On evenings that David Rockefeller and his family dined at Blue Hill, conversation with the Barbers turned naturally to farming and food, in particular, sustainable agriculture. The Rockefellers' suggestion that their farm in Pocantico Hills might be a great place to practice sustainable agriculture soon evolved into the Stone Barns Center for Food and Agriculture. Part of this enterprise was a second Blue Hill restaurant that brings the field to the plate. Diners at Blue Hill at Stone Barns experience *terroir* firsthand. They enjoy grass-fed lamb or fresh lima beans as they gaze out over lush pastures and gardens. The cuisine at both restaurants is a "clean, pure homage to nature's remarkable bequests."

Sustainable agricultural includes seasonality. Dan's recipe for pistou is a perfect example of a dish that can be adapted to the four seasons. The base can be fresh peas in the spring, zucchini in the summer, soy beans in the fall, and root vegetables in the winter. The goat cheese with faro crackers adds a luxuriousness to the dish and carries the richness of the vegetable base. "This is a dish," Dan says, "I often enjoy eating at home."

Chef Dan Barber — Blue Hill Restaurant, New York, New York

Pistou of Summer Veggies with Goat Cheese and Faro Cracker

SERVES ⟩ 4

PISTOU INGREDIENTS:

10 medium asparagus spears (about 6 ounces), trimmed and cut into ½-inch pieces

1 cup (3 ounces) sugar snap peas

1½ pounds fresh fava beans (or fresh soy or lima beans, depending on availability)

4 cups fresh basil leaves, loosely packed

¾ cup extra-virgin olive oil

1 small shallot, finely chopped

1½ cups vegetable stock or canned vegetable broth

½ teaspoon fine sea salt

½ teaspoon freshly ground black pepper

FARO CRACKERS INGREDIENTS:

1 cup faro

1 cup whole milk

3 cups water

1 cup coconut milk

Pinch of salt

GOAT CHEESE SPREAD INGREDIENTS:

8 ounces chèvre, plain, at room temperature

2 tablespoons sherry vinegar

2 shallots, diced small

1 tablespoon olive oil

1 tablespoon fresh cream

3 tablespoons fresh mixed herbs such as chervil, chives, oregano, and parsley, coarsely chopped

Salt and pepper to taste

GOAT CHEESE SPREAD DIRECTIONS:

⟩ Using an electric blender, whip all the ingredients together.

⟩ To serve, ladle pistou into bowls and sprinkle each with the herb mixture. Serve with faro crackers and goat cheese spread.

PISTOU DIRECTIONS:

⟩ In a medium saucepan over high heat, bring salted water to boil. Have ready a large bowl of ice water.

⟩ Blanch asparagus and snap peas separately for about 2 to 3 minutes, or until the vegetables are just tender. Immediately remove each vegetable from the pot and shock in the bowl of iced water. Drain and pat dry.

⟩ Repeat process with fava beans, blanching for about 1 minute. Drain and slip the outer skin off each fava bean. Discard skins.

⟩ Repeat the process with the basil, blanching for about 45 seconds. Spread on paper towels to dry.

⟩ In a large bowl, combine the blanched vegetables. Transfer half of the vegetable mixture to a blender and add the basil. Blend until chopped, then add 5 tablespoons olive oil in a slow, steady stream, and puree until smooth.

⟩ In a heavy, large saucepan, over medium-high heat, heat remaining 1 tablespoon olive oil. Add shallot and sauté until translucent, 3 to 5 minutes. Stir in vegetable stock, vegetable puree, and the remaining blanched vegetables, salt, and pepper, and bring to a simmer. Cook, stirring occasionally, until vegetables are heated through (3 to 5 minutes).

FARO CRACKERS DIRECTIONS:

⟩ Place all ingredients in a medium saucepot and bring to a simmer.

⟩ When the faro is very soft, and overcooked, remove from heat and puree in a food processor.

⟩ Spread the mixture onto a Silpat baking mat with an offset, very thin spatula.

⟩ Place in a preheated, 250°F, oven for about 1½ hours.

⟩ Remove from oven and, using a knife, cut into small rectangles, about 1 x 4 inches. Return to oven and continue cooking for about 3 more hours, or until the crackers are brittle.

⟩ Store extra crackers in an airtight container.

Crème Fraîche Potato Gratin

SERVES > 6

INGREDIENTS:

1 ounce cultured butter lightly salted
3 leeks, white and a little of the green parts only, sliced
  in half lengthwise, cleaned, and chopped
2 cloves garlic, minced
Salt and freshly ground pepper to taste
1 tablespoon fresh thyme, chopped
1½ cups whole milk
8 ounces crème fraîche
4 pounds Yukon Gold potatoes, peeled and sliced thin
1 cup cheddar or gruyère, grated

DIRECTIONS:

> Preheat oven to 400°F.

> Melt butter in a large sauté pan over medium heat. Add leeks and garlic, stirring occasionally to allow the leeks to become somewhat translucent and caramelized. Add salt, pepper, thyme, and milk, and allow to come to a boil, stirring frequently. Lower heat and stir in the crème fraîche.

> Add the sliced potatoes and allow to simmer for a few minutes. Make sure to gently stir the potatoes so all are coated. Butter a 10- x 14-inch gratin or casserole dish, and pour the potatoes and cream sauce into it. Sprinkle with the cheese, and bake for 1 hour, until potatoes are soft.

Vermont Cheddar

With all of the cheese trading in Vermont, we eat a lot of Vermont potato gratin. We choose sharp Vermont Cheddar that is white and aged to perfection. Our favorites are Cabot Creamery, Shelburne Farms, Grafton Village Cheese Company, and Neighborly Farms of Randolph, Vermont.

Grilled New York Strip Steaks with Coupole and Fig Demi-Glaze

SERVES ⟩ 4

STEAK SAUCE INGREDIENTS:

½ cup fig jam or spread
¾ cup port wine
1 cup unsalted beef broth

STEAK INGREDIENTS:

4 New York strip steaks or sirloin strip steaks
Salt and freshly ground pepper to taste
1 Coupole

DIRECTIONS:

⟩ Start sauce a half hour before grilling.

⟩ Put the fig jam, port wine, and beef broth together in a small saucepan and bring to a boil. Turn heat down to medium-low and simmer, stirring occasionally, until it has reduced by half.

⟩ Meanwhile, light the grill and remove steaks from the packages. Salt and pepper steaks on both sides and grill to your liking.

⟩ One minute before the steaks are finished, place a slice of Coupole on each steak and close the lid until the cheese starts to melt and steaks are done. Allow steak to rest at room temperature for 5 minutes before serving. Taste the sauce and add salt and pepper if necessary. Serve with the sauce on the side or drizzled over the top.

 ## The *Affinage*

Affinage, French for "aging," applies to cheese, wine, meat products, or olive oil. The *affinage* in cheesemaking is the final step. It builds flavor, changes textures, and enhances the characteristics of a cheese. Bonne Bouche, Bijou, and Coupole age for one to two weeks in our aging room and then will continue to age in their packaging up to two to three months, depending on your preference and taste. The temperature, humidity, ventilation, cheese flipping, and composition of the air are the most important factors in the *affinage* process. Parmigiano Reggiano or Comté cheese can be aged for up to two years; cheddar, up to five years!

Fresh Crottin-Stuffed Leg of Lamb

SERVES › 8

SPINACH STUFFING INGREDIENTS:

⅓ cup olive oil

1 cup red onions, minced

12 ounces prewashed baby spinach, chopped

¼ cup fresh parsley, chopped

1 tablespoon salt

⅛ teaspoon freshly ground pepper

¼ cup pine nuts

½ cup sun-dried tomatoes packed in oil, drained
  and chopped

4 ounces Fresh Crottin (about 1 cup), crumbled

LAMB INGREDIENTS:

1 leg of lamb (5 to 7 pounds), trimmed, boned,
  and patted dry

¼ cup olive oil

3 tablespoons fresh lemon juice

2 large garlic cloves, minced

1 tablespoon fresh thyme, chopped

2 teaspoons salt

½ teaspoon freshly ground pepper

2 cups hot water

SPINACH STUFFING DIRECTIONS:

› Heat oil in a large skillet over medium-high heat. Add onion and sauté until soft, about 10 minutes. Add spinach and parsley and sauté about 2 more minutes. Remove from heat and stir in pine nuts, sun-dried tomatoes, salt, pepper, and Fresh Crottin.

LAMB DIRECTIONS:

› Preheat oven to 350°F.

› Place lamb skin-side down on work surface. Flatten slightly. Combine ¼ cup olive oil, lemon juice, garlic, thyme, salt, and pepper in a small bowl and beat well with a fork.

› Rub half of oil mixture over the top of the lamb. Then spread the spinach mixture over the top of the lamb. Starting at the shank end, fold a third of the meat over, then fold the leg portion over the top (as for a business letter). Tie with string, starting at the thicker end and using slipknots to form a roll enclosing the stuffing. Close cavities at ends with a threaded larding needle. Rub outside thoroughly with remaining oil mixture.

› Transfer the meat to a large roasting pan. Add 1 cup hot water. Roast, basting frequently, until a meat thermometer inserted into the thickest part of the meat registers the desired degree of doneness (about 2 hours for medium). Add more hot water to pan as necessary to prevent drippings from burning.

› Transfer lamb to a serving platter and let stand several minutes before carving. Strain drippings and ladle sauce over the meat.

Desserts

On a hot summer evening, there is something sublime about churning your own ice cream in the backyard. A copious supply of crème fraîche, a flat of luscious, ripe red strawberries or deep purple blackberries, and an old-fashioned hand-crank ice-cream maker delivers the season. When the berries arrive, and ripen by the quart, we're ready to churn the cream. For weeks every adult, child, and Labrador retriever who visits the farm gorges on the succulent windfall. Good and decadent. Remy and Cloé in the photo can attest. With every click of the camera they became more intoxicated, feasting on the strawberry crème fraîche dasher at the end. When tasting Molly's cherry ice cream, I felt like one of the kids — I couldn't get enough of it — not to mention the cupcakes!

To take advantage of summer fruit, if we're not churning crème fraîche, we're rolling out butter pie crust. It is the greatest complement you can give to flavorful fruit.

Afraid of dessert and pastry? Fear not. They couldn't be easier and are risk free with really good ingredients: high-fat cultured butter, creamy mascarpone, and nutty, thick crème fraîche. Imagine inhaling the fragrances of a flaky apple pie or *tarte tatin* hot from the oven on a crisp fall day, or tasting the luxurious flavors of a mascarpone cheesecake, or being enticed into a holiday kitchen by the heavenly aroma of freshly baked butter cookies spread with velvet chocolate ganache. Yes, dessert can be decadent and filled with our favorite culinary aromas that transport us to great memories of celebration, family rituals, and tradition.

Bijou Crème Brûlée with Rhubarb Compote

INGREDIENTS:

3 Bijou
1 quart milk
½ quart cream
Salt and white pepper to taste
10 egg yolks
3 whole eggs
Half bunch fresh thyme, chopped
6 tablespoons raw sugar for caramelizing the brûlée
1 pound rhubarb, peeled
1 pound strawberries, stemmed
1 cup granulated sugar
½ teaspoon vanilla extract
½ teaspoon lemon juice

DIRECTIONS:

› Cut the Bijou in pieces, add to milk and cream with salt and pepper, and warm in saucepan, but not to the point of boiling. Put aside. In a bowl, put the egg yolks and whole eggs, mix together, then add a pinch of salt and pepper and the chopped fresh thyme.

› Carefully combine both mixtures and then slowly mix together using a hand blender. Season to taste. Pour the custard into crème brûlée containers and bake in the oven in a water bath at 275°F for 30 minutes until firm.

› Let cool, and then just before serving, burn with raw sugar under the broiler or with a torch.

SYRUP DIRECTIONS:

› Dice rhubarb and strawberries and put in a pot with sugar, vanilla extract, and lemon juice. Cook for 10 minutes until it has a compote-thick consistency. Cool and serve at room temperature as a quenelle (teaspoon) on top of the crème brûlée.

 ## Culinary Students Experiment

Chef Adrian Westrope, pastry chef and instructor at the New England Culinary Institute in Montpelier, Vermont, easily rose to our challenge of making a crème brûlée using goat cheese!

The talented student team worked with two different cheeses: our Fresh Crottin and aged Bijou. They creatively mixed the cheese in the custard, melted it in a pan, or crumbled it over the brûlée before baking. This resulting recipe balances sweet and sour, and pairs brilliantly with the acidity of the strawberry compote. No wonder NECI has been voted among the top three culinary schools in the United States.

Chef Molly Hanson

GRILL 23 & BAR, BOSTON, MASSACHUSETTS

The seed of Molly Hanson's career as one of New England's foremost pastry chefs was possibly planted as a child, when she accompanied her father as he collected honey from his beehives. To this day, Molly helps her father keep bees. "When you extract honey," she says, "it is exciting and messy and intensely fragrant. The smell of the honey is incredible."

A little like bees, Molly has migrated from place to place, gathering her skills and developing her repertoire. She began at the New England Culinary Institute in Vermont. Her internship took her to San Francisco and a little "mom and pop" restaurant where she started out making savory items like quiches and pâtés, but when the pastry chef "didn't work out," she was asked to take over that job, too. She fell in love with pastry.

When she returned to Vermont, she found a position working under Chef Tom Bivins at Shelburne Farms, the beautiful late-nineteenth-century Vanderbilt-Webb estate turned inn, restaurant, and working farm. Then it was back to San Francisco and a stint at Mark Franz's Farallon restaurant and an opportunity to work with the dynamic Emily Luchetti, an extraordinary pastry chef.

Missing her family and New England's lushness, Molly finally returned to Boston. She took a position as the pastry chef at Harvest in Cambridge, creating seasonal desserts that reflected the freshness of New England. "We had a lot of fun doing classic New England desserts

Molly Hansen, Grill 23 & Bar

like 'Brown Betty,' a sort of cobbler" she recalls. Today Molly is still buzzing around experimenting with flavors and textures and working as the pastry chef at Boston's Grill 23 where she is serving up scrape-your-plate delicious desserts.

While working at Farallon, Molly learned more about one of Emily's favorite ingredients — mascarpone. "Emily uses it in everything!" Molly notes. "And so it was natural that it played a starring role for me in the beginning of developing my desserts." In her cheesecakes, Molly says, "It lightens it more than cream cheese, and it is truly versatile. I serve it straight or occasionally sweeten it and add a little vanilla. This is lovely with almost any dessert from chocolate cake to a fruit crisp. And it is a great filling for anything from cupcakes to cookies." And indeed, mascarpone is an ingredient in Molly's superb "Devil's Food Chocolate Cupcakes" recipe. The other ingredient that she uses is crème fraîche, which "has a richer flavor than heavy cream. It also adds a sweet tanginess, but doesn't go as far as sour cream or yogurt." With a simple ice cream accompaniment that has not only crème fraîche but griottines — very fine marinated French cherries — friends and family will linger around the table for quite a while enjoying this truly decadent dessert.

Chef Molly Hanson—Grill 23 & Bar, Boston, Massachusetts

Devil's Food Chocolate Cupcakes with Crème Fraîche Cherry Ice Cream

MAKES › 15 cupcakes, 1½ quarts ice cream

ICE CREAM INGREDIENTS:

24 ounces crème fraîche
3 cups whole milk
1 cup sugar
1 vanilla bean
1 tablespoon vanilla extract
¼ cup high-quality marinated cherries, such as griottines

CUPCAKES INGREDIENTS:

1¼ cups all-purpose flour
¾ cup cocoa powder
1¼ cups sugar
2 teaspoons baking soda
½ teaspoon baking powder
2 large eggs
2 ounces crème fraîche
½ cup milk
¼ cup canola oil
1 teaspoon vanilla extract
¾ cup warm coffee

CUPCAKE FILLING INGREDIENTS:

6 ounces mascarpone
¼ cup heavy cream
1 tablespoon sugar
½ teaspoon vanilla extract or about one-third of a
    vanilla bean (seeds only)
Whip all ingredients together until soft peaks form.
    Keep refrigerated until needed.

GANACHE INGREDIENTS:

4 ounces semisweet chocolate (60%)
4 ounces crème fraîche

ICE CREAM DIRECTIONS:

› Blend all of the ingredients, except for the cherries, and freeze in ice-cream freezer according to directions. Once the ice cream is churned (after about 35 minutes), add the strained cherries and 3 tablespoons of the cherry liqueur syrup. Run the churn just long enough to distribute the cherries in the ice cream.

› Place in containers and store in the freezer. Ice cream will become hard after several hours.

CUPCAKES DIRECTIONS:

› Preheat oven to 350°F.

› Sift dry ingredients into a large bowl. Whisk eggs, crème fraîche, milk, oil, vanilla, and coffee in a separate bowl. Add egg mixture to the dry ingredients, whisking well to break up any lumps.

› Line muffin pans with paper or foil liners. Fill pans three-quarters full and bake 15 to 20 minutes, until a knife inserted in the center of the cakes comes out clean. Cool the pans for 10 minutes, then turn out onto wire racks.

FINISHING:

› Melt chocolate in a double boiler. Whisk in crème fraîche until smooth. Ganache will set up quickly so do not make this until you are ready to use it.

› Prepare a pastry bag with a ¼-inch tip filled with mascarpone filling. Insert the tip of the bag deep into the cupcake and fill until it bulges out the top. Fill all of the cupcakes.

› Fit the pastry bag with a ½-inch star tip with the crème fraîche ganache and garnish the top of each cupcake, or frost the cupcakes with a spatula.

› Note: If you don't want to add the ganache, simply use all 8 ounces of the mascarpone and garnish the top of the cupcakes with the filling.

The French *Tarte aux Fraises*

INGREDIENTS:

16 ounces fromage blanc
1 tablespoon lemon zest
2 eggs
2 egg yolks
½ cup sugar
1 baked tart crust (use your favorite; see box below)
2 cups assorted fresh berries

DIRECTIONS:

> Preheat oven to 350°F.

> Mix together all ingredients, except the berries, and fill one 9-inch pie tart shell or four 6-inch tart shells with the mixture. Bake 10 to 15 minutes until just slightly brown around the edges and almost set. Remove from oven and cool to room temperature or refrigerate overnight.

> Arrange berries on top before serving, glaze with apricot jam (mixed with a little hot water if needed) or sprinkle with confectionary sugar.

Easy Pie in the Sky

Making your own pie shell can be the deal-breaker for luscious tarts. Here are some ways you can avoid the pie crust struggle: Buy the crust. Some good ready-made crusts are now available in specialty stores or supermarkets. We recommend the pie shell from our friends at Vermont Mystic Pie.

If you insist on making your own crust, here is an easy recipe:

1 ¼ cups all-purpose flour
¼ teaspoon salt
4 ounces cultured butter unsalted, chilled and diced
¼ cup ice water

> In a large bowl, combine flour and salt. Cut in the butter until the mixture resembles coarse crumbs. Stir in water, a tablespoon at a time, until mixture forms a ball, but don't overwork the dough. Wrap in plastic and refrigerate for 4 hours or overnight.

Vermont Mystic Pie Company

Apricot Almond Butter Biscotti

MAKES > 24 biscotti

INGREDIENTS:

3½ cups all-purpose flour
1½ cups sugar
2 teaspoons baking powder
½ teaspoon salt
1 pinch nutmeg
8 ounces cultured butter unsalted, cold
2 cups almonds, chopped fine
2 cups dried apricots, chopped
4 eggs
1½ teaspoons vanilla extract
1 tablespoon orange zest
4 sheet pans covered with parchment paper

OPTIONAL:

6 ounces white chocolate, melted
1 cup sliced almonds for decoration

DIRECTIONS:

> Preheat oven to 350°F.

> Combine all dry ingredients in a bowl, including the sugar. Cut cold butter into small pieces and add to the dry ingredients. Using your fingers or a pastry cutter, rub the butter into the dry ingredients until it is the texture of chunky cornmeal. Add the chopped almonds and apricots to the dry ingredients.

> In another bowl, whisk together the eggs, orange zest, and vanilla. Add eggs to the flour mixture and fold gently until the dough is formed together. It's okay if it is a little sticky. (If the crust is too dry, add a small amount of ice water to bring it together.)

> Turn dough out on a floured surface and form into long cylinder-shaped logs. Place on the parchment paper and flatten slightly.

> Bake at 350°F for 25 to 30 minutes, until light brown. Remove from oven and cool completely.

> Using a bread knife, slice the biscotti diagonally in pieces ⅓ inch wide. Place on parchment and bake again for 15 to 20 minutes at 350°F, until lightly toasted.

OPTIONAL:

> Dip biscotti in melted white chocolate and sliced almonds and allow to set. (For gentle boiling use doubleboiler.)

> The biscotti can be kept in an airtight container for up to 10 days.

ASSORTED COOKIE PLATE

Butter Pecan Icebox Cookies

INGREDIENTS:

8 ounces cultured butter lightly salted
½ cup brown sugar
½ cup sugar
1 large egg
½ tablespoon vanilla extract
2¼ cups all-purpose flour
1½ teaspoons baking powder
½ teaspoon salt
1 cup pecans, toasted and chopped fine

COATING MIX INGREDIENTS:

Mix the following items together and set aside to roll the dough in later:
1 cup pecans, toasted and chopped fine
½ cup sugar
½ teaspoon ground cinnamon

DIRECTIONS:

› Using an electric mixer, beat butter and sugars until creamy. Gradually add egg and vanilla until incorporated. Combine flour, baking powder, and salt, and add to butter mixture, beating well at medium speed. Stir in 1 cup pecans.

› Shape dough into two 6-inch logs. Sprinkle pecan, sugar, and cinnamon mixture on a cutting board and roll the logs of dough in it. Wrap logs in waxed paper and refrigerate overnight.

› Remove dough from the refrigerator and slice into ¼-inch slices.

› Place slices on a sheet pan lined with parchment paper and sprinkle with sugar before putting in the oven. Bake cookies at 350°F for 12 to 14 minutes, until light brown. Remove cookies and cool on wire racks.

ASSORTED COOKIE PLATE

Vermont True Decadence Brownies

INGREDIENTS:

10 ounces unsweetened chocolate
16 ounces cultured butter lightly salted
9 eggs
4½ cups sugar
1 tablespoon vanilla extract
8 ounces crème fraîche
2¼ cups all-purpose flour
12 ounces of semisweet or dark chocolate chips

DIRECTIONS:

❯ Preheat oven to 300°F.

❯ Grease a 13- x 18-inch sheet pan.

❯ Melt chocolate and butter in a double boiler over low heat, then cool to room temperature.

❯ Whisk eggs slightly, then add sugar, vanilla extract, and crème fraîche. Mix until incorporated.

❯ Fold chocolate and butter mixture into the egg and sugar mixture, alternating with the flour in 2 parts. Do not over mix! Fold in chocolate chips.

❯ Bake for 45 to 50 minutes. You will want these brownies to be slightly gooey. Cut brownies into 2-inch squares.

❯ Note: For a thicker brownie, use a 9- x 13-inch pan.

Four Season Mascarpone Cheesecake

CRUST INGREDIENTS:

2 cups shortbread-cookie or graham-cracker crumbs
(16 ounces)

3 tablespoons cultured butter lightly salted,
melted and cooled

FILLING INGREDIENTS:

32 ounces mascarpone
1¼ cups sugar
4 large eggs
2 egg yolks
1 tablespoon vanilla extract

DIRECTIONS:

› Preheat oven to 350°F.

› Tightly wrap the outside of a 9-inch springform pan with foil and set aside. Prepare the crust by placing shortbread-cookie or graham-cracker crumbs and butter in a food processor and pulsing until it is the texture of rough cornmeal. Press crumb mixture into the bottom of the pan and one-third of the way up the sides of the pan. Bake until light brown, 10 to 12 minutes. Cool to room temperature.

› Using an electric mixer, beat the mascarpone and sugar on medium for just a few minutes, until light and fluffy. Continue to mix on low, adding the eggs one by one and the yolks until incorporated, then add the vanilla extract.

› Scrape down the sides of the bowl with a rubber spatula and mix on medium for 30 seconds. Pour filling into pan with cooled crust, and place in a large roasting pan. Pour enough warm water in the roasting pan to come halfway up the sides of the springform pan.

› Bake for 1 hour and 15 minutes. Turn off the oven and leave cheesecake in the oven with the door ajar for 1 more hour.

› Remove from oven and finish cooling cheesecake on a wire rack to room temperature.

› Refrigerate for at least 8 hours before serving.

 ## Seasonal Variations

Winter: *Grand Marnier Cheesecake*: Replace the vanilla extract with 2 tablespoons of Grand Marnier and 1 tablespoon of orange zest. Use chocolate cookies for the crust.

Spring: *Lemon Cheesecake with Blueberry:* Add 2 tablespoons of lemon zest and 1 tablespoon of lemon juice to the filling. For the crust, use 1½ cups of shortbread cookie mixed with ½ cup of ground almonds and 3 tablespoons of butter. Serve with blueberry compote.

Summer: *Vanilla Bean Cheesecake:* Slice 2 vanilla beans in half and scrape the seeds from the beans into the batter. Serve with fresh summer peaches and raspberries.

Fall: *Cinnamon Spice Cheesecake:* Add 1 tablespoon of cinnamon and 1 teaspoon of nutmeg to the batter. Serve with warm apple compote. Use ginger snaps for the crust.

Index